Junie Moon Rising

A true story.
A hedonistic woman tries to change so she can
adopt a child from the streets of Asia.

JUNE COLLINS

PARTRIDGE
A Penguin Random House Company

To order additional copies of this book, contact
Toll Free 800 101 2657 (Singapore)
Toll Free 1 800 81 7340 (Malaysia)
orders.singapore@partridgepublishing.com

www.partridgepublishing.com/singapore

Previous Books by author;

The Khaki Mafia . . .
By June Collins and Robin Moore

Goodbye Junie Moon
By June Collins

DEDICATION

I dedicate this book to my children. They will not recognize the mother they know, but then children rarely do know the person submerged beneath the role of 'mother'.

AUTHOR'S NOTE

This book contains a small amount of profanity. Such was life and dialogue as I knew it so I make no apologies but offer the warning. I have also taken liberties with time in order to 'move the story along'. However, the events of my memoirs are true and in chronological order to the best of my recollection (which is exceptionally good).

CHAPTER 1

Washington D.C.

I awoke from the sleep of the dead. For a few seconds, my mind was blank and I stared uncomprehendingly at the unfamiliar hotel room. Then the events of the past seventy-two hours flooded back. I glanced at the built-in digital clock on the bedside table and realized I had slept for fourteen hours. Jet lag had finally caught up with me. Nervous tension had kept it at bay for a couple of days. Now, my testimony before the U.S. Senate Subcommittee on Investigations was behind me and I felt as if a weight had been lifted from my shoulders. I sat up, my mind screening a rerun of recent events like a familiar old movie.

Safe at last! Done! Finished! Over! Only days earlier, I had been in Vietnam, scared to leave because I'd been told the airport was being watched. But despite having a price on my head, I had escaped. Two days after arriving in the USA, I had testified before the Senate Committee and, by yesterday, my photo had been splashed over the front pages of every newspaper in the country. The story went worldwide and I was labeled a whistleblower . . . a heroine.

Senator Abraham Ribicoff, Acting Chairman of The Senate Committee, had publicly praised me saying, "You are not an American but you did a great service for this country when you risked everything to bring this 'Khaki Cosa Nostra' to justice."

I didn't let any of it go to my head. The title of heroine was balanced by my enemies who called me a whore. I didn't feel like a heroine and I knew I wasn't a whore. Let them call me what they would. I knew I was just an ordinary person, intrepid enough to follow my fate.

But that was all behind me now. The future loomed emptily ahead; my business as a booking agent bringing entertainment to the troops in Vietnam was destroyed.

I climbed out of bed wearing only my panties. Shivering in the unfamiliar coldness of air conditioning, I stumbled to the bathroom and climbed gratefully into the white, fluffy chenille robe provided by the hotel. I thought about the 'bad guys' I had testified against. They had wanted me dead so I couldn't talk. But I *had* talked and the world had listened. Surely there was no reason to kill me now, was there? They would be the first suspects. Still, it might be best if I remained alert.

In two more days, I needed to vacate this hotel room, which the committee had paid for, along with my ticket out of Vietnam. I should have felt elated that I had beaten those crooked army club sergeants yet I felt terribly flat. It reminded me of the big letdown that often follows Christmas and I recalled an army chaplain once telling me that there were more suicides in January than in any other month.

I had one tiny glimmer of hope. Two nights earlier, after seeing me on the evening news, a writer named Robin Moore had phoned from New York and suggested a book collaboration. I grabbed onto the idea like a drowning man clutches a rope.

I ordered room service and was waiting for my scrambled eggs and toast to arrive when Robin Moore phoned me for the second time. He suggested I check into Manhattan's Barbizon Hotel for Young Women at Lexington and 53rd Street East.

"My condo is on 72nd near Lexington," he said. "It's convenient to have you nearby."

"A hostel for young women isn't exactly my style." Absently, I twirled a strand of blonde hair around my finger.

"It won't be for long. Besides, it was good enough for Joan Crawford, Ali MacGraw, and Rita Hayworth." His voice sounded sexy.

"Well, if a firecracker like Rita Hayworth could handle it, I guess I can." I laughed.

"I could get you a discount at The Sheraton Hotel." Robin paused. "Father was the founder of The Sheraton chain, you know. His first three acquisitions were right here in New York but, even with a discount, it would cost more than the Barbizon. I'm sure money's tight after losing your business."

"You got that right." I digested his information before asking, "Do you work in the family business then?"

"The Sheraton? Not anymore. Father took a partner, added four more hotels then sold out. I handled the P.R. My first book, 'Pitchman', was based on those P.R. days. After selling it, I quit the hotels and I've been writing ever since."

Wondering if he looked as attractive as he sounded, I replied, "I read your book, 'The Green Berets.' It was terrific."

"Thanks. Look, Junie Moon, I gotta run. In the morning, you head to the Washington airport and take the shuttle to La Guardia. They leave every hour. Take a cab to the Barbizon and I'll meet you in the foyer at seven tomorrow night. Gentlemen aren't allowed above the ground floor so do be ready."

"Yes, Mr. Moore. I'm looking forward to meeting you."

"It's Robin, remember. We're going to be seeing a lot of each other while working together so forget this Mister stuff."

"Yes, Robin. Any suggestions on what I should wear tomorrow night?"

"Well certainly not army fatigues. I'll make a reservation at Twenty One."

After hanging up, I sat on the edge of the bed and mentally replayed our conversation, trying not to get too excited. Book royalties could alleviate my precarious financial situation and give me a fresh start. I clung tenuously to an unfulfilled promise made years earlier, a promise to take one of those small Asian beggars off the streets. My conscience nagged me with the passing of time but maybe I could do that now. However, one thing was certain: I would need to change my ways and live a more normal life. My past had been anything but normal.

When breakfast arrived, I thanked the waiter and ate without tasting; my mind preoccupied with things other than food. While washing the lukewarm toast down with strong coffee, I absently noticed the vase of dying carnations. They had been a 'Welcome to the USA' bouquet from the two senate investigators. I couldn't bear anything dead around me. Leaping up, I threw them into the wastebasket then turned my attention to clothes. I had left Vietnam with only one small suitcase. Apart from the circumstances of my hasty departure, I hadn't needed a huge wardrobe over there. For three and a half years, I had worn army fatigues most of the time.

Opening the closet door, I looked at the conservative, brown woolen dress I had bought to wear at the hearings. That would have to do. My first trip to New York or not, even I had heard of Twenty One, that very 'in' restaurant. To an ordinary girl, a sheep farmer's ex-wife, this was pretty heady stuff.

CHAPTER 2

New York

The following day, I arrived in Manhattan to discover that November in New York was equally as cold and damp as Washington. Peering from the cab window, I wondered why New York was called 'The Big Apple'. It seemed such a meaningless sobriquet.

The cabbie screeched to a halt in front of a tall, red brick building. I handed him the amount registered on the meter and his smile disappeared. Apparently he expected a tip, a custom we had not yet adopted in Australia. Reluctantly, I handed over more money.

With my high heels clicking noisily over the polished floor, I carried my suitcase across the depressing and silent reception area. At the check-in desk, the spinster-type receptionist peered at me above wire-rimmed glasses.

"We've kept a room for you on the fifth floor, Miss Collins. And, please remember, no gentlemen callers past reception and the doors are locked at twelve sharp." Her expression clearly indicated she expected me to test all the rules. This was not the welcome I had become accustomed to. During the flight, the airline hostess had recognized me from earlier newspaper headlines and greeted me warmly.

I shrugged and took the elevator to my narrow, simply furnished room. Dimly lit by a forty-watt bulb, it was as cold as the receptionist downstairs. What on earth had Rita Hayworth been thinking of?

With hours to kill before meeting Robin, I decided to explore that Big Apple.

I hung up my few clothes, tucked my hair inside a beret, then headed for the wintry outdoors. Just as I stepped onto the street, a car backfired, causing me to flinch. That's an improvement, I thought, resisting the urge to throw myself to the ground, a reaction developed after too many mortar attacks.

Braced against the cold, I wandered wide-eyed along Lexington Avenue, absorbing the throbbing vitality of the city. Stern-faced pedestrians brushed past me; everyone seemed to be in such a hurry. Winter's drab colors were brightened by a sea of cheery yellow cabs which clogged the road, stopping and starting in spurts. Sleet and light snow drifted and quickly evaporated, sprinkling my face. I found the sensation invigorating, all my senses on alert. Clouds of steam billowed up from grates in the sidewalk, briefly warming my legs. This was such a contrast to the heat and vivid colors of the tropics, yet the very difference was exciting.

Mouth-watering fragrances of ground coffee beans and freshly baked bread wafted out from the many delicatessens. Street vendors in woolly caps and scarves sold hot pretzels from stands along the pavements. Wondering what they tasted like, I tried one but, finding it dry and too salty, I threw it into the gutter.

My cheeks were turning stiff from the cold and my belly rumbled. A window full of olives and hanging pastrami lured me into its black-and-white tiled interior. This new experience, new place, demanded a new taste thrill. I settled for a Reuben sandwich and ate with relish as a sliver of sauerkraut escaped onto my chin.

By 7:00 p.m., I was apprehensively waiting in the foyer for Robin of the sexy phone voice. When a conservatively dressed, middle-aged man with thinning hair approached, my expectations plummeted.

"Junie Moon. What a pleasure." He kissed me on each cheek, his warm greeting slightly dispelling my disappointment. The Marlboro Man he was not, but, as the night progressed, he proved to be fascinating company.

"Now, about our working arrangement," he said, after the waiter removed our dessert dishes. "My attorney, Marty Heller, wants us both in his office tomorrow so he can prepare a contract. I'm ready to start working on the story outline immediately."

"Where?" I asked.

"Well not at my place, that's for sure. My wife Liz is going to scream blue murder when she gets an eyeful of you." He had been drinking steadily throughout the meal and now gazed a little too openly at my breasts. "I have a studio down on 42nd Street where I write when I'm in town. I prefer writing at my Jamaican property but, at the moment, I need to stay here. My latest book, 'The French Connection', is being made into a movie and they're shooting it in New York. You'll find the studio pretty basic but you can stay there while we're writing."

"Basic or not, I have a hunch I'll like it better than the Barbizon. Which reminds me, I'd better get back or I might be locked out."

Robin's face fell.

CHAPTER 3

Unforgettable Vietnam

"Ya gotta live it up to write it down." Robin grinned as he entered the studio and flopped onto the daybed. His long, daily 'business lunches' were cutting into our writing time.

"You've been telling me that for the last three months," I grumbled, irritated that he was late again.

"Now, now, Junie Moon. Just a little nap and I'll be ready to work for another two hours."

I looked at the clock and frowned. It was already three o'clock. If he slept for an hour and then we worked for two more, by five his wife Liz would be phoning every few minutes as she always did if he was late.

I admired Robin's courage. In order to write 'The Green Berets', he had undergone jump training with The Special Forces at Fort Bragg. He then received special permission to go to Vietnam with them for six months, gathering material for that book.

But I was anxious to get on with my life and he kept returning late and glassy-eyed from lunch. If he worked overtime, both Liz and his girlfriend harassed me with endless phone calls.

Already he was snoring lightly, his mouth slightly agape, his graying hair rumpled against a cushion. What did all these women see in him? His little black book bulged with female names and far too many phoned. Obviously, his writing studio had a dual purpose.

Until he woke up, I couldn't do much for I wrote under his guidance. Robin plotted the book and wrote the segments about the Senate investigation; I wrote the sections about my involvement leading up to the hearings. Using his old Remington typewriter, he inserted my chapters, editing as he went. He was calling our story 'faction', fiction based upon facts.

Wandering disconsolately to the kitchenette, I poured another coffee. Until the book was sold, I was broke so haste was imperative.

My exhilaration over bringing the crooked army sergeants to justice had been short-lived. At first, I had enjoyed all the public attention. When my picture hit the newspaper front pages, I became Queen for a Day—a temporary diversion for the New York social set who briefly embraced my differences. Yet I couldn't overcome the feeling of being a Martian, not belonging anywhere.

Initially, I was awestruck by the glitter and glamour of New York's high society but soon the superficiality galled me. Designer labels and the 'in crowd' seemed irrelevant. I was lugging the invisible baggage of Vietnam with me and the memories hadn't dissolved with a snap of my fingers. They overflowed my brain. They ached in my heart. They cowered under my skin.

I had been living one 'life' one minute then, after a few short hours on a plane, I was thrust into an entirely different one. The sudden contrast was overwhelming.

While writing about Vietnam all day, it was impossible to forget and move on. As the initial excitement generated by the hearings quieted, depression began creeping up on me— stealthily—like a cheetah stalking a gazelle.

Nothing felt real anymore. In Vietnam, the GIs used to talk longingly about returning to the *real* world. But eventually that place of war became *our* reality. I wondered if many of them, upon returning to that so-called 'real world', felt as alien as I did. Possibly not as much, I assumed, considering they were returning to their own country. Yet, how else could that sea of lost souls known as Vietnam veterans be explained? And would I have felt any different had I returned to Australia? I concluded many of us must have lost our sense of belonging to the place we left because those of us who returned were no longer the same people.

Robin's depressing little brown studio with its strident telephone was no help. It sat above The 13 Coins Chinese restaurant and the nauseating cooking fumes frequently seeped in. At night, I smelled the odor clinging to my pillowcase. While I tossed and turned on the narrow daybed, Robin was ensconced in his luxury, high-rise condo. Liz had decorated it with zebra-skin covered floors, mirrored walls, and countless vases filled with armfuls of white lilies.

In search of sleep, I began medicating on wine and sleeping pills. I could understand why Vietnam vets suffered this way but why me? I had not been in combat.

Life remained unpredictable. Short term, there was the book to finish but what then? I still toyed with the idea of adoption but over the last few years, my zeal had faded, impeded by too many obstacles; little things, such as the war. However, I had made enquiries at a New York adoption agency, only to be told that it was impossible for single women to adopt. Liberal changes allowing 'singles' and homosexuals to adopt were many years down the road.

I wanted to keep my promise to take one of those Asian street children, but, long ago in Australia, I swore I would never marry again. I planned to finish my life very happily as a single woman. Thoughts of children had been shoved strongly off my radar . . . until that night in Manila when I saw those little beggars asleep on the sidewalk and my heart broke. The sight of their soiled, crumpled bodies flashed to mind. The eldest no older than maybe eight; newspaper used in place of sheets; and the huge, hairy, red-eyed rat that scurried away from the soles of their feet at my approach.

Putting down my empty coffee cup, I noisily tidied the kitchen, hoping to wake Robin. He didn't stir but I heard a sound outside the door. Opening it, I found no one there. But, from the corner of my eye, I caught a glimpse of a black, flowing skirt disappearing around the corner. My foot brushed against something. I bent and picked up a small, rag doll riddled with pins.

"Not another one," I mumbled, slamming the door and throwing the gift from Robin's girlfriend into the garbage can.

Robin had introduced us the previous week when she broke his rule of no uninvited guests at the studio. She had stared at me from granite-hard eyes as she wrapped her arms possessively around Robin's waist. Tall and thin, she towered above him and her long, black hair fell across his shoulders.

"Did Robin tell you I'm a witch?" she rasped. "You keep your hands off my man if you know what's good for you."

I had laughed aloud, my respect for Robin plummeting. "Well, hop on your broomstick and fly away. I'm busy."

Robin got rid of her and returned, shoulders hunched, avoiding my eyes.

Being new in the U.S. and after living removed from western civilization for years, I didn't always understand what was happening around me. When Robin took me to The Friars Club, an exclusive men's hangout for the rich and famous, I was unaware that I was meant to be impressed.

Four or five of us sat drinking while a chatty group at the next table fawned around an older man. He openly stared at me before inviting Robin to bring 'his friends' and join his table. Robin eagerly complied, seating me beside the lascivious celebrity. The man's wit kept his audience in peals of laughter but he did not interest me. My rebuff embarrassed all present. Robin quietly scolded me for being rude to such a famous television personality.

Living in Vietnam, where we had only limited Armed Forces Network Television, I had never heard of him so, to me, he was just an unattractive, old man. Such experiences reinforced my feeling of being a Martian. 'Their' values were not mine.

Years later, Charlie Daniels recorded a song called 'Still in Saigon.' The lyrics perfectly described me in those early New York days. How could I forget Vietnam when it was still so fresh in my mind and I wrote about it all day?

My moods swung between boisterous laughter and thinly-controlled anger. On a good day, I hid my feelings; on a bad day, I had none. No anger, no fear, no sadness, no joy, no lust. I felt like 'Dead (wo)Man Walking'. I was physically, mentally and sexually defunct. During one of those days, I stepped out into Manhattan's rush-hour traffic against the lights. Amid squealing brakes and screamed abuse, I ambled zombie-like to the other side, numbly daring death. I felt so dead that there was no motivation to do anything, even to take my own life . . . or to save it.

Then a few weeks later, I picked up the newspaper and read a small article about Jurate Kazickas, a journalist with AP. While covering the war in Vietnam, she became famous among the Marines. They affectionately nicknamed her, possibly due to her height of six feet, Big Sam. Frequently, she was the first reporter to jump off a chopper following a battle, striding over the body-strewn fields even before the mop-up. In 1968, while on a field operation with the marines, she was wounded in the battle of Khe Sanh.

The article said she had attempted suicide in a gas oven. I was shocked. I had recently bumped into her in New York. She was riding a bicycle through Manhattan, curly hair and cotton skirt flying in the wind. When I hailed her, she rode over and we went for coffee. There was no indication anything was wrong. She was still reporting for AP but, somehow, she seemed as out of place as I felt.

Deeply affected by her attempted suicide, I did some research and discovered that more Army nurses suffered depression after Vietnam than after any previous war. (And any war since—I've recently learned.) I can't say enough about my admiration for those dedicated women. The realization that one is participating in a futile war where tens of thousands of young men are dying needlessly is devastating. Nurses had to deal daily with the death and dying which I did not. But my knowledge of the dying and my involvement with the corruption had eroded my spirit. After reading about the nurses, I oddly felt better. Not due to lack of compassion, but because I knew I was not alone.

By day, Robin and I were busily writing; by night, we were being lavishly entertained. Liz was always there, clinging possessively to Robin. Clearly, she didn't like me. Young, big-busted blondes are seldom popular with other women, especially if they are locked in a small space with the woman's husband all day.

We mingled with interesting people. We lunched with Harold Robbins, the hottest author of the day. We had coffee with Barbara Walters. She was charming and wanted to interview me on morning television but her producer said 'no', he hadn't believed my story. At the New York Explorer's Club, I was enchanted by the seafaring adventures of Thor Heyerdahl of the Kon Tiki expedition. Since age ten, when I fell in love with Gulliver, I was always drawn to adventurers.

Many weekends, I explored New York alone. I climbed the steps inside the Statue of Liberty—all the way up to the torch—in the days before terrorism banned that activity. I took the elevator to the top of the Empire State Building where I swayed and felt dizzy. I traveled by ferry to Staten Island. I wandered through Central Park and sipped tea at The Plaza's Palm Court. Just another gawking tourist.

I managed to control my drinking in public until one night when Robin, Liz, and I were invited to join a few of his friends for dinner at an exclusive new restaurant.

Seven of us entered the elegant room on ankle-deep carpet. Rich tapestries hung on brick walls beneath soaring ceilings; timber shone warmly and crystal sparkled. The strains from a violin quartet added ambiance to the muted atmosphere. Yet it failed to lift my spirits after a day of writing about things which still stirred my emotions.

A tuxedo-clad waiter placed a napkin on my lap then poured Cristal champagne into a hollow-stemmed goblet. I absently thanked him, lost in morbid thoughts. My dinner companions made polite conversation but I did not participate. What did I care about the latest Broadway show or their new physical fitness trainers?

Staring morosely at the bouncing bubbles in my glass, I quickly squelched their effervescent dance with a big gulp. The efficient waiter repeatedly filled my goblet. The surrounding opulence only increased my despair as a series of vignettes sprang unbidden to mind. When the waiter sat a dish of pink prime rib before me, I saw flashes of young soldiers, squatting in torrential rain, hunched beneath oilskin ponchos while eating C-rations from khaki-colored tins. I shoved my plate aside, untouched. I did not belong here with these bejeweled and fur-clad ladies. Emptying my glass, I slammed it down, breaking the stem. Quick as a whiplash, I leaped onto the center of our table with a wounded scream. Wine goblets and china cups toppled over. Glaring angrily around the room, I pointed an accusing finger at the diners, never considering some could have sons in Vietnam.

"What's wrong with you people?" I screamed. "Don't you have any feelings? Don't you care that your young men are out there in the mud dying for you while you're pampering yourselves? You disgust me."

Robin frenziedly tugged my skirt while waiters rushed towards us. They dragged me down, threw me out into the street and banned me forever. I wasn't their 'type'. Robin was gentlemanly enough to escort me back to the studio and I vaguely remember him and Liz leaving.

I wish I didn't remember staggering to the neighborhood cocktail lounge after they left. The bartender decently tried to stop me from drinking more but I craved oblivion. My earlier explosion hadn't alleviated my turbulence; it only added a twisted remorse to my seething anger. I made eye contact with a good-looking (I think), dark-haired man. He helped me back to the studio and I dragged him into bed. Popping amyl nitrates, I tried to bring my dead libido back to life, clawing and writhing my way through the next half hour. The ferocity of my attack turned his initial pleasure to anger and he removed his bleeding body with a few harsh words then left, slamming the door.

Stumbling to the shower, I turned it on full force, so hot it scalded me. Falling against the tiled wall, I slid in a cloud of steam to the floor and lay there, pelted by water which coursed around me before gurgling down the drain. Then I cried . . . and cried.

The next morning when Robin arrived and found the empty pill bottle, he phoned a doctor friend. I opened my eyes, confused, and looked around before recognizing the studio. The previous night's events flooded back like dirty water. I groaned. I had only made things worse.

"How are you feeling now?" Robin asked after the doctor had reprimanded me with a few threats about Bellevue and then left. I turned my head to the wall, not answering; not wanting him to look at me.

"Luckily, I came in early," he said.

"Just leave me alone."

"Junie Moon, you have a problem, honey. I think you need to get away from New York. How would you feel about going to Jamaica and finishing the book in Port Antonio? It's peaceful there."

CHAPTER 4

Another Fresh Start

A week later, I sat on the plane trying not to think about the behavior responsible for this trip. My outburst and self-degradation were best forgotten. As my mother always said, "You can't unscramble eggs."

I cleared my mind by focusing on Robin who was in exuberant spirits. He wandered, drink in hand, up and down the aisle, chatting and joking with the Jamaican passengers in childlike happiness which I found endearing. He was never so carefree in New York although I had noticed his eyes lit up whenever he spoke of Jamaica. Liz was matching him drink for drink but looked petulant. I remained guiltily silent, 'on the wagon'.

At the Kingston airport, Robin's caretaker, Julius, was waiting beside an old Chevrolet sedan. We loaded the luggage and left immediately for Port Antonio. Thirty minutes into our trip, the last of Kingston's shantytown houses disappeared, replaced by a dazzlingly lush, tropical landscape.

"This is more my style." I smiled at Robin.

"We know your style!" Liz snarled.

Many travel writers, then and now, have extolled Port Antonio's natural beauty. It sits off the beaten track but attracts the world's wealthy. Today, although its heyday of hosting royalty and movie stars has passed, it remains peaceful and uncrowded. Most tourists traipse to the more familiar destinations of Montego Bay or Ocho Rios on the opposite side of the island.

In 1970, Port Antonio was a very small community indeed, home to a cheerful Jamaican community and a handful of semi-permanent Caucasians. Most of the Caucasians were wealthy English who spent summers on their inherited estates.

Our arrival coincided with the seasonal return of the gentry. As we approached our destination, I stared in admiration at the glistening white homes and sparkling swimming pools dotting the hills. They sat amid verdant gardens of bougainvillea and palms, overlooking spectacular views of the sparkling ocean.

"I've owned The Blue Hole for many years," Robin volunteered as Julius slowed down. "These homes belong to friends of mine. You'll meet many of them while you're here."

"Jamaicans, too?" I prodded.

"Of course! There's no racism here."

I raised an eyebrow. The mood in America at that time was changing. Robin was one of the many whites appalled by the treatment of African/Americans. Yet even while he called for 'equality', he was not averse to laughing at a racial joke. Like so many of his class, his liberalism was tinged by an unconscious air of superiority towards other races and people of lower social strata. After all, he was a Harvard graduate, a proud achievement occasionally flaunted.

There was little variety to his generous wardrobe of conservative Brooks Brothers suits, routinely accessorized with the old school tie. So while I never considered Robin a racist, he was definitely a Wasp, (white Anglo-Saxon protestant), smug in his benevolent whiteness and family background.

We passed a sign reading "Fairy Hill" and Julius parked the car on the side of the road.

"Home!" Robin sighed contentedly.

"I thought you lived in Port Antonio. What's this Fairy Hill?"

"It's the outskirts of Port Antonio. We're not in the town proper."

"Yeah! There are no men around here to keep you company." Liz sneered as we grabbed the luggage.

"Quit it, Liz! We are going to be stuck together every day, so give it a break."

Robin and Julius took the largest suitcases and we set out in single file down the narrow, hillside path.

"A real rain forest. What a paradise," I said, following along.

"I live in the top house," Robin volunteered. "You go with Julius to the writing studio a little further down. It doubles as a guest cottage. His wife or one of his boys will come in and straighten up each morning."

Liz shrugged. "I'm ready for a drink."

"Now, now, Liz dear. Let's unpack first."

We stopped beside Robin's cottage. Birds squawked overhead and blue water glistened through the palms further down the track.

"Julius runs The Tea House at the bottom of the hill. We'll catch you down there beside the lagoon in an hour."

He and Liz left and, moments later, Julius unlocked the door to my temporary home.

The simple guest cottage, enclosed within glass louvers, was an improvement over the place above the Chinese restaurant. The air smelled of earth and flora, not deep-frying fat.

I clattered noisily across bare boards to the small bedroom where a mosquito net hung above a white, iron bed. A couple of geckos played tag on the planked walls. I threw myself onto the bed and lay there, in no hurry to move.

After unpacking and taking a shower, I followed the path to The Blue Hole. Liz and Robin were already there, drinking pina coladas while bathed in the kaleidoscopic colors of a magnificent sunset. Nearby, a fire pit emitted mouth-watering aromas of sizzling pork. The cheerful sounds of reggae music drifted across the lagoon.

"Who owns The Tea House?" I asked, observing several Jamaicans sitting outside the nearby thatched structure.

"The property's all mine," Robin began, "but I . . ."

"Yours and mine!" Liz interrupted.

"But I lease The Tea House to Julius and his family," Robin said, ignoring his wife. "They make a decent living and take good care of my place. I like my privacy so I keep The Tea House separated inside the fence. Customers have the view but not the use of the lagoon."

Moments later, one of Julius's well muscled teen-age sons appeared carrying a flaming torch.

"Hullo, Mr. Boss." He grinned at Robin. "I chase away mosquitoes." He passed on bare feet and lit the bamboo flares around the water's edge. I watched his progress, quietly admiring his well-developed abs until Robin caught me and I blushed. Wisps of black smoke rose in the evening air, tinging it briefly with kerosene fumes. The yellow flames grew brighter, their flickering light dancing across the darkening water. I sighed heavily; the romantic setting made me wish I wasn't just a third spoke in the wheel. It had been a long time since any thoughts of romance had entered my head.

"In the past, I rented this place out as a movie location," Robin interrupted my thoughts. "It was used as location for one of Robin Williams's movies. A little later, Brooke Shields made it famous with her movie, 'The Blue Lagoon'. Everyone started calling it The Blue Lagoon then and the name stuck. The older folk still call it The Blue Hole and claim it's bottomless." His voice softened. "Wait until tomorrow. When the sun hits it at different angles, it changes color between aquamarine, turquoise and sapphire."

"Oh shut up with the travelogue," Liz snapped. "Isn't it time Julius brought another round?"

Back in the cottage, my first night was restless. No sooner did I fall asleep than a huge crash made me leap up, yelling "Incoming!" A heavy object thumped noisily down the corrugated grooves of the metal roof before smashing into the gutter and shooting out to the ground below. Within moments, I realized the sound had come from a coconut falling onto the tin roof. That sound would disturb my sleep many times in the coming weeks.

Robin and I were early risers. Neither of us ate breakfast and, by the time he knocked on my door at seven a.m., I had the coffee ready and we commenced writing. The house was not air-conditioned and we avoided the midday heat by taking a long lunch break with Liz joining us beside the lagoon.

After lunch, she and Robin took turns skiing across the sparkling water with one of Julius's boys at the boat helm. They both possessed the grace and skill of elite athletes. Surprised by, and envious of, their talent, I worked on my tan, drawing lascivious glances from Robin. If I lounged too close to the water's edge, Liz delighted in skiing close to shore. After turning sharp and fast, drenching me beneath a watery fountain, she flashed away, her laughter spinning out across the lagoon. Her intent backfired one day when Robin ran forward and enfolded me in a huge fluffy towel, holding me in his arms long enough to infuriate Liz.

"Can't you ski, Junie Moon?" he asked, one day. I shook my head, 'no', and Liz smirked. Thanks to Robin's flirting, her jealousy had reached alarming proportions. I suspected Robin deliberately provoked her insecurities and I occasionally felt sorry for her. I had considered trying to befriend her but she was too mean to me. Briefly, I thought of exchanging my skimpy bathing suit for something less revealing but Liz, too, followed the current rage and wore a tiny bikini. Unfortunately for Liz, by cultivating that "New York Thin" look, she had lost her behind. Whenever she entered the lagoon, her bikini pants filled with air and bobbed on the water's surface like a floating balloon.

"I'll have to teach you to ski, Junie Moon." Robin grinned. "There's no time like the present."

Although I had been a professional dancer for many years, I was surprised to find myself completely hopeless on skis. I spent more time under water than on top. When I surfaced, choking up water and with my nose running, the sight afforded uproarious entertainment for Liz. The Jamaican tearoom customers, upon hearing Liz's merriment, turned to stare, their voices soon joining hers in raucous laughter.

Following lunch, Robin and Liz routinely returned home so Robin could take an hour's siesta—or so he said. I suspected Liz owed me a debt of gratitude. While Robin 'rested', I took long, lonesome walks through the rain forest. Sweating in the humidity, I often stopped by one of the scenic waterfalls, to stoop and drink the crystal-clear liquid. It never occurred to me that, in years to come, people would waste money *buying* water to carry everywhere, as if embarking on a trek through the desert.

One afternoon, while wending my way back to the guest house, I stopped to enjoy the wonderful song of a nearby bird. I looked up, searching the branches of the surrounding trees. Slivers of sunshine splashed my upturned face. I inhaled deeply and was stunned by a thought. I was happy!

CHAPTER 5

Fairy Hill, Jamaica

Frenchman's Cove, the neighboring property, was an exclusive resort comprising forty-five waterfront acres of magnificently landscaped tropical gardens. Queen Elizabeth and the Duke of Edinburgh took holidays there. So did Princess Margaret and countless other heads of state and movie royalty.

Frequently, as we sat around The Blue Lagoon enjoying our evening cocktails, the resort owners zigzagged through the palm trees in their open-topped jeep to join us. They were a friendly couple who usually dressed in khaki shorts and shirts with pith helmets. I half expected to see them drag in a dead tiger or two. Despite the congenial evenings, I was always the odd man out, both by having no escort and by my continual sense of 'never fitting in'. My recovery and growing happiness was a solitary thing.

Grainger Weston was the son of Garfield Weston, otherwise known as The Cookie King of Canada. The "Who's Who" of this world meant nothing to me but they were nice people. When Robin told me that his own family was included in the American "Who's Who", I responded with a shrug of my shoulders. My mother had always raised her children to judge a person by their character, not by material wealth or social standing.

Sitting around the lagoon at sunset, eating pit-roasted, crackling pork from greasy fingers and slurping up exotic cocktails, I was experiencing 'the good life'. Night and day, the exotic sounds of reggae music burst forth from The Tea House distracting me with its rhythm. It had been a long time since I had really danced. Pleasant as our evening rituals were, as time passed, I longed to slip away and join the 'poor natives' who were letting it all hang out, grooving to the beat.

The seventies were so different! You either belonged to a 'white' segment or a 'black' segment and the two rarely mixed.

One night, the music's temptation became too great. After Liz and Robin retired, I snuck down to The Tea House. With Julius and family bound by secrecy, it became a nightly event. I was, of course, the only white customer. Sweat-soaked and happy, I managed to get a few hours sleep each morning before writing again. For me, dance was always a passion and passion of any kind had been missing for too long.

I suspected Robin guessed my nocturnal habits after I too began taking afternoon naps. He probably thought it was all about 'nookie' for he had never known the thrill of uninhibited dance, being imprisoned by the sedate 'white man's' shuffle. Respectable people weren't supposed to let their hair down the way Rita Hayworth did. Or the way Ava Gardner did, or the way I sometimes did. Music and dance were bringing me back into the human race.

It was a Saturday morning and we seldom wrote on weekends.

"Do you want to come for a ride with me, Junie Moon?" Robin asked.

"Where to? Is Liz coming?"

"She's still sleeping. I'm going to buy some eggs. The old guy is in his eighties but you might find him interesting."

"Sure. I'll come," I replied.

After a fifteen-minute drive, Robin turned the old sedan off the road and, with the engine laboring, we drove up a perilously steep, rutted, dirt driveway. Reaching the top, he spun the car around to face downhill then pulled up in a cloud of dust and spurting gravel before cutting the engine. As we got out of the car, fowls ran underfoot in the unkempt garden at the rear of a run-down, timber house with sagging shutters. A large, meaty Jamaican woman with a mahogany face worn out from life was hanging clothes on the line. I estimated she was in her sixties and I marveled at her hair which was thick and shiny black, pulled back into a loose braid like that of a young girl.

Squinting into the sun, she yanked a wooden clothes peg from her mouth and called out, "Hullo, Mr. Moore. I'll be with you in a minute." She had that musical rise and fall of the Jamaican accent which I loved.

"No hurry," Robin replied. "Where is Mr. Jackson today? Is he sleeping?"

"No. He's sitting on the front porch, enjoying the view."

Robin frowned. "How can he enjoy the view? He's blind."

"As a bat," she agreed, continuing to hang the clothes. "The Parkinson's getting worse but still he likes to look out towards the ocean. He said the smell of the ocean brings the pictures back to his mind from the days when he could see it."

Her poignant comments touched me. "That is beautiful but also sad," I said. She ignored me as though I was an impertinent stranger, lacking the right to speak.

"This is my houseguest, June Collins," Robin made the introduction. Mrs. Jackson nodded brusquely, possibly considering mundane courtesies a waste of time.

"Here after some eggs are you?"

"Yeah."

"They're not layin' as many these days but I'll see if I can rustle up a dozen." She finished hanging the last garment and wiped her large hands on her apron.

"Do you mind if I take June around the front of the house to meet Mr. Jackson? I told her all about him being from England and fighting in World War I and she would like to meet him. She has recently come from the war in Vietnam."

"He don't like visitors these days. Says they all talk nonsense and he can't be bothered."

"We'll leave if we seem to be bothering him."

She spat, expertly aiming her gob of saliva onto a busy ant mound. "Go take your chances then."

As we walked around the side of the house I asked Robin, "Are there many mixed-race marriages out here?"

"Very few. The Jackson's settled in England at the end of WWI but his family disowned him so he moved out here." He cut off what he was saying and abruptly grabbed my elbow, steering me around a pad of cow dung which I hadn't noticed. "Racism was worse than what it is now," he said.

"I hope it's been worth it."

"Who wouldn't be better off out here than in England? Look!" We had rounded a corner and the vista spread before us caused me to stop and inhale sharply. I had seen this magnificent shoreline and sparkling ocean almost daily but never from this height with an unobstructed 360-degree angle. On the horizon behind me, the lush, wildly beautiful Blue Mountains rode the range beneath a blue sky streaked with filmy ribbons of cloud. In the foreground, a tumult of bougainvillea spread exuberant in a profusion of purples, reds and cyclamen, almost too vivid for my eyes. To one side soared a sea of swaying palms interspersed by Poinciana trees laden heavy with tangerine blossoms. Umbrella trees, taro and wild bananas ran rampant above a carpet of feathery ferns.

At the furthest point forward, coves of snowy white half-moons framed the azure water of the ocean which dazzled with a billion spangles of sunlight. My eyes misted over. How could anyone become jaded with such a view? The old people's house may have seen better days but their property atop Port Antonio's highest peak would be a developer's dream. I cringed at the thought of mere mortals tampering with nature's magnificence, all for money.

"I wish I had brought my camera," I whispered, filled with spiritual delight. Robin gazed at me, enjoying my reaction. His scrutiny felt like an intrusion.

"Who's there?" rasped a quavering voice from off to my right.

"It's Robin, Mr. Jackson. I've got a young lady with me and she wants to meet you."

"Why would she want to meet me?" He grumbled in a voice grown gravelly from too many years of smoking cigarettes. However, belying his lack of welcome, he reached for his walking cane and rose stiffly from the bench where he sat then turned in our direction. He was tall and angular, the frame of his shoulder bones sticking out gauntly like a coat-hanger as they held up his shirt. He wore clean but crumpled cotton shorts, a short-sleeved, buttoned-down shirt and leather sandals. A nose grown prominent with time dominated his creased face and cloudy eyes seemed to peer at a point just above my head.

"My name's June and I hoped we might exchange a few war stories if you like," I said, stepping up to him and lightly touching his free hand. He fumbled then turned his hand to clasp mine before shaking it. The veins of his spindly arms stood out darkly like purple threads behind his crinkled, sun-parched skin. His knuckles were huge mounds of calcified bone and his skin felt like cracked leather as he pumped my hand in a surprisingly firm grasp.

"Come and sit beside me if you have nothing better to do, young lady," he said, the harshness fading from his voice.

"I'll go around and talk to Mrs. Jackson," Robin interjected. "I'll see you soon."

The old man and I sat on the bench in comfortable silence. Eventually he started the conversation and it soon became apparent there was an intangible connection between us. Any age barrier dissolved, if indeed it had ever existed, as he enthralled me with his stories about fighting the Germans and the Turks during WWI. I was a bit of a war history buff and he soon made it clear he held a great deal of admiration for the Turks, even though they had been his enemy.

"They were such fine soldiers," he said. "And the Germans, their so-called allies, treated them like dirt. One time I remember, the combined German and Turk forces were overrunning our position. To breach the coils of barbed wire along our perimeter, the Germans ordered the Turks to throw themselves upon the wire, enabling the Krauts to stampede over them."

Fate must have brought us together. I shared his admiration of the Turks and had read many military history books about their performance during the Korean War.

"When I was living in Korea," I told him, "I dated the Turkish charge-d'affaires. He often took me to visit the Turks at their camp on the DMZ at Panmunjom. Their camp was poor, their vehicles and equipment old, in sharp contrast to the nearby American camp. However, whereas the Americans had numerous guards to stop the local thieves, the Turks had none. They told me that when they caught thieves, they cut their hands off. It may seem harsh, especially as the Koreans were dirt poor, but it worked. Theirs was the only camp not being robbed." I brushed away an annoying fly and continued. "So I don't know about WW1, Mr. Jackson, but I do know that in the Korean War the Turks alone never lost a prisoner in the POW camps. Prisoners of other nationalities ridiculed them, calling them animals for eating dirt and grass. The Turks understood the earth's mineral content and they alone survived intact."

Mr. Jackson's voice quavered. "They were tough but they always fought fair." He coughed hard for a moment and his hands shook. I reached across and took one bony hand in my own, gently holding his thin, cold fingers as I would a small child. My touch startled him but he did not immediately pull back. The shaking eased.

Soon Robin was calling me to leave. I followed the old man out of the sunshine as he led the way, tapping his cane through the darkened house. The living room was filled with heavy, old-fashioned furniture and along one wall were shelves holding hundreds of books.

"You must have enjoyed reading," I commented.

"I miss that most of all." Nostalgia crept into his gravelly voice.

"Maybe I can rectify that. I have free time every afternoon. How about I have one of the Jamaican boys drive me over here and I read to you? Have you read 'Uhuru' or 'The Honey Badger' by Robert Ruark?"

Soon after, I left, knowing I had made a friend. He felt 'real' to me, as so many others still did not.

CHAPTER 6

Bad Dreams

A bad dream woke me at three a.m. Such dreams were fading but, just when I thought they were gone, back they came. This one was familiar. I was crouched behind a very small rock dodging bullets. As I buried into the dirt, scratching at it with my toes and wishing it would open up and swallow me, my heart pounded. The bullets pinged all around, following me as I scuffled about behind that little rock. When I awoke, hunched in a tight coil, my heart still thumped against my chest.

It was useless going back to sleep; I might only resume the dream. Instead, I stumbled to the kitchen and made a cup of coffee. As the brew bubbled and filled the room with its tantalizing aroma, I picked up the previous day's work and started reading it. The story was coming along well. I had tried focusing on all the good times, such as when I ran The Waltzing Matilda, my club in Nha Trang. Finishing the coffee, I made a few corrections. Whenever I turned my pages over to Robin, he made any necessary alterations before typing them up on his old Remington. He always said a book had to be written and rewritten . . . and rewritten.

Robin, Liz and I dined at a local hotel that evening. The Jamaican owner bustled to our table to greet Robin. While they chatted, a young man approached. He was the epitome of tall, dark and handsome. The owner introduced him as his son, Thomas, explaining that he was seldom home, being a commercial airline pilot who flew to and from the States.

The music started and Thomas invited me to dance. I left my food unfinished and glided around the dance floor in the tall man's arms. He guided me with the confidence he must have acquired from flying a plane. Hotel guests stared and my spirits soared as his musky after-shave titillated my senses.

An hour later, as Robin rose to leave, I looked at him and said "I'm staying Robin. I'll see you in the morning."

"But how will you get home?" he frowned.

"Taxi!" I muttered as Liz shook her head.

Thomas and I danced until the wee hours of the morning when we ran to the hotel's deserted beach and threw our hot bodies into the surf. Yellow moonbeams fell like a shower of buttercups upon the gently swelling, dark water. We laughed and splashed, as playful as dolphins. When he rose from the water, towering darkly above me, the heat from his body warmed my flesh in the chill night air. Laughter died in my throat as my long dormant libido awoke. I slid my hands up his chest, reaching for his face. A night bird called out from the darkly silhouetted palm trees just as his firm hands grasped my buttocks. He hoisted me up to his lips and I wrapped my legs around his hips, no longer hearing that night bird or the water lapping on the sand, only the symphony filling my head.

Eventually, we waded back to shore and continued our lovemaking on the beach until, sated, I fell asleep. Within seconds, he was shaking me awake. The first rays of daylight streaked the sky.

"Quick," he said. "We have to move before someone comes out and catches us."

Brushing the sand off my body, I flung my clothes on. "Can we meet tonight?" I asked, knowing a relationship between us would raise a few eyebrows amid the white community.

"Who's gonna stop us?" he growled.

Robin and I were nearing the completion of our book. He informed Liz and me at lunch one day that he was flying back to New York for a brief business meeting. I wondered if 'The Witch' was calling.

"I'm coming with you," Liz exclaimed. "I won't stay here with her." She pointed at me.

"Sorry dear. Not this time. I'll be busy and you will only slow me down. I'll be back in three days."

I was as unhappy as Liz about being left alone together. My pilot had flown to the States and wasn't due back for days. There was only so much sunbathing and solitary jungle walks one could endure.

Two days after Robin left, I stupidly made the mistake of going to bed without locking the door of the guest house.

When The Tea House closed at night, Liz and I were the only two people for miles around. Port Antonio was seven miles north and Frenchman's Cove a mile further south.

I tried to read by the dim bedroom light. An army of geckos was playing, noisily contemptuous of my presence. Jamaican geckos emit a strange 'ack, ack' sound not conducive to sleep and they were adeptly dodging the shoes I hurled at them. It must have been around eleven o'clock when they scampered away and I fell asleep.

Liz had obviously been drinking when she burst into the cottage, trumpeting like a charging elephant. She rushed towards the bed, slashing the air with a machete. Still half asleep, I managed to throw myself onto the floor, barely dodging the machete before it sliced into the mattress. I scrambled to my feet, by then fully awake, and ran into the living room with her hot on my heels. Stopping long enough to grab a bar stool, I hurled it in her direction and made my escape.

I ran barefoot through the jungle wearing nothing but panties. Hadn't I warned Robin not to leave her behind? Amazingly, although she was drunk, she seemed to be gaining on me.

Whoosh! Whoosh! The sounds of the machete were audible above my labored breathing as she cut a swath through the tangled jungle vines. With pounding heart, I struggled through the underbrush as large plantain leaves slapped against my sweating face. A twisted vine caught my foot and I stumbled forward. My pace slowed while I tried to regain my balance before crashing head first into the trunk of a palm tree. I could hear Liz yelling, "Where are you bitch? Come out! Come out wherever you are!"

I scrambled behind the trunk of the palm tree which had stopped my flight, but had given me a splitting headache. The cloud that covered the moon, making my dash so hazardous, now worked to my advantage. I cowered in impenetrable darkness beneath the ferns and bracken which sprouted below the palm tree. Liz stopped only feet away and I held my breath. The night seemed uncannily still.

Even in the hands of a drunk, that machete could do harm. I squeezed myself into a tight ball as blood trickled from a gash in my forehead. Nearby, a coconut dropped with a heavy thud onto the dense leaf bed of the jungle floor. My gasp almost gave me away.

While mosquitoes feasted hungrily on my sweaty skin in the muggy air, Liz cursed and searched blindly. Plop, plop! A large, raindrop coursed through the leafy canopy and splattered onto my forehead. The crack of thunder shook the ground as a sudden deluge punched fiercely into the gigantic taro leaves. Their shiny surfaces shook and quivered like a Hawaiian dancer's grass skirt. Lightning lit the jungle, and waking birds screeched. Throaty frogs hollered and cicadas joined in, their volume swelling and falling, washing over me in deafening waves.

Surely Liz would leave now? We couldn't stay drenched outside all night. My knees had grown stiff from crouching. I was about to confront her when she screamed, "You're no fucking hero! You won't face me, so stay out here and rot, you whore!"

She turned on her heel and was gone.

"How did I end up in this shit?" I wondered. "Can't I ever meet normal people anymore? Won't my life ever return to normal?"

When I saw the distant slits of light appear through the shutters of Robin's cottage, I stood. Clumsily, I slipped and slithered downhill with mud squelching between my toes. The rain stopped as abruptly as it had started and clouds drifted away, revealing a weak, partial moon amid a sky full of water-hazed stars. I kicked the guest house door open then slammed it. This time I braced a chair beneath the knob.

"That whoremonger's gonna get a piece of my mind when he returns," I mumbled, reaching for a towel.

The joy of sunshine.

CHAPTER 7

Sad Memories

Does everyone question their purpose for living, I wondered? I was sitting on the sand at Half Moon Bay. There was no wind and the waves rolling in were small. A little further down the almost deserted beach, a dark-skinned woman sat, watching her two small children playing on the water's edge. I, too, watched the children. Robin was due back in the afternoon. Meantime, I was steering clear of Liz. Between the clanging coconuts throughout the night, my bad dreams had returned.

The Jamaican children set me thinking of years past when I had given birth to my own three babies. Two of them were technically miscarriages but—at five and a half months—to me, they were births. Little Heather, born premature at seven months, would have been almost thirteen now. She only lived for five hours and the doctors had never let me see her—or hold her.

My husband and mother-in-law had that privilege but I never even got to see a photograph—or attend her funeral. I was still in the hospital and no one told me she was buried until after they returned from her graveside. Later, I sprinkled violets over her grave.

Those years of teen-age marriage to the Australian sheep farmer seemed like another life, one that had happened to another person.

Normally I avoided such pensive thoughts but, contemplating my approaching birthday, I was reflective. In the sixties and seventies, it was customary for women my age to be already married with a family. As for divorce, it was almost unheard of with statistics standing at 2%. I was one of that 2%. Where was I heading? I thought of the men I had loved and discarded. In Vietnam, I had fallen hard for one colonel. Where was he now? No doubt he was enjoying life with his family.

Was I wrong when I swore I'd never marry again? I adored men's company but not on a permanent basis. My own family's history made me cynical about love and marriage. I had proved I could take care of myself but sometimes it grew lonely. Robin and Liz's relationship further cemented my views on marriage. They shared no trust or harmony; offered each other no support. Luckily, they spawned no children to traumatize. And there it was again . . . children. That was the goal I had failed to reach.

Again, I glanced at the two small, black children frolicking on the water's edge. And, again, my mind harked back to the horror I felt that night when I saw those little Filipina girls sleeping on the Manila sidewalk, so vulnerable to predators. That moment of epiphany! I promised to change and return to take at least one of them off the streets. Yet almost seven years had passed. Was I all heart and no action?

There were so many excuses, like the dancing years when I partied hard and spent all my money on fine jewelry. I could have taken one then but I had rationalized that I couldn't drag a child all over Asia, living out of a suitcase.

In Hong Kong, while on R&R from Vietnam, I had compromised by finding Amy, a beautiful little Eurasian girl. She lived with her fat, Chinese grandmother. For years, I had given the grasping old woman money to educate and take good care of Amy. On my many visits in and out of Hong Kong, I had spent most of my days with Amy, buying her pretty dresses, reading her stories. She always cried when I left, begging me to take her with me. But how could I take her back to Vietnam? I promised to return for her when the war, my war, was over. Too late I discovered the old woman was a phony. She had bought Amy with plans to get rich by selling the child to a wealthy businessman as soon as the girl was ripe. It was the superstition of wealthy Chinese that bedding a young virgin meant prosperity in the coming year. By the time I learned this, the woman had disappeared, taking Amy with her.

Amy's beautiful face still fills me with regret whenever I look at her photograph and wonder, what sort of a life did she end up having.

I had tried assuaging my guilty conscience by taking the eleven-year-old Vietnamese boy, Dong, off the streets of Nha Trang. He was a wily child whom I wrote about in Goodbye Junie Moon. Dong was not like a child at all, after being exposed to life on the streets for too long. We had not bonded and he objected to the restrictions I placed on him; things such as showering and attending school. Eventually, he ran back to the freedom of the streets.

I sighed heavily, my gaze still following the two Jamaican children. Excuses, excuses! My dreams of adoption had begun fading. There was no point reaching for the moon. I had no husband, no money and—I hated to admit it—emotionally, I was still pretty unstable.

Attracting men was never a problem. There had always been a bevy of backstage admirers. Before Vietnam, which I referred to as B.V., I was outgoing with a great sense of humor which was now in recovery. I dressed glamorously, expensively, and walked with a dancer's grace. According to 60's and 70's thinking, women like me were considered great mistress material. For marriage, men sought modest, submissive women with 'the-girl-next-door' looks and excellent homemaking skills. Changes nowadays are like comparing Doris Day to Lady Ga Ga.

Enviously, I watched the mother call her children back. When she stood and wrapped their small, wet bodies in towels, I left the beach.

Back at The Blue Lagoon, I discovered Robin had returned from New York. He laughed when I told him about my harrowing night with Liz. No doubt it added to his repertoire of amusing cocktail party stories. The thought crossed my mind that he thrived on other people's turmoil, possibly looking for material to use in future books.

"The sale of our book is a wrap," he informed me. "I want to finish it and leave here in two more weeks. I've got other fish to fry."

We were invited to dinner at Patrice Wymore's house on our last night in Jamaica. Patrice, tall and coolly elegant, was one of my favorite Port Antonio people.

She leased a dress boutique in The Trident Hotel which she and her husband, the Australian actor, Errol Flynn, had once owned. Unfortunately, Errol's drug habit left them short of money and the hotel was sold, leaving her with nothing but the boutique.

She and Errol first met while making a film together. She, a young, newcomer to Hollywood, fell head over heels in love with the swashbuckling star. They married and, while sailing on his beloved yacht, dropped anchor in Port Antonio and fell in love with the place. The Trident was only one of several real estate investments they made before settling down to live happily ever after on a large waterfront coconut plantation. Unfortunately, as the old adage goes, "the best plans of mice and men . . ."

It was to the rambling house on the coconut plantation that we headed, with Robin at the wheel of the old sedan.

I wore a long, white skirt and fuchsia-colored linen jacket. Robin wore his favorite yachting jacket and gray flannel trousers, having left the Brooks Brothers suits back in New York. Liz was subdued in black.

The houseboy opened the door and mouth-watering aromas welcomed us. Patrice appeared, untying her apron.

"I've prepared dinner myself." She smiled, patting down her blonde, upswept hairdo. "I hope you like tarragon chicken in white wine and mushrooms."

"My favorite." Robin was at his most gallant.

During the meal, Patrice spoke about the problems caused by a virus killing many of the coconut trees. It forced her to fly back and forth to Las Vegas to raise money, doing casino shows.

Throughout dinner, her teen-age daughter, Arnell, picked sullenly at her food, ignoring us. We drank brandy with our coffee while Robin kept us amused with stories about Sonny Grosso, the New York cop depicted in 'The French Connection.' He said that during his recent trip, Sonny had introduced him to a madam named Zaviera Hollander. We all laughed as the story unfolded. All except Liz.

"Who knows? I might write her story next," Robin said, eliciting a further glare from Liz.

FOOTNOTE:

For those old enough to remember, a few years earlier, Errol had gone on a drug bout. Suddenly disappearing, he had abandoned Patrice and the plantation. He surfaced in France with a sixteen-year-old girl. Feeding his escalating morphine habit, he sold his much-loved yacht and anything he could get his hands on. Only Patrice's court action saved the plantation. After the drugs killed him, his teen-age girlfriend laid claim to that. The case dragged through the courts, making headlines until Patrice won.

During my years in Vietnam, I often heard journalists speak with admiration of Errol's son, Sean. He was a young journalist who tried to make it on his own, never using his father's name or his influential connections. However, possibly trying to live up to his father's daredevil reputation, he was known as a risk-taker. By the time I met Patrice, Sean had disappeared while chasing a story in Cambodia. His body has never been recovered.

Arnell, the petulant daughter, was probably already a junkie that night of the dinner. She caused Patrice years of heartache and—while still in her early thirties—she, too, died of an overdose. Her body was found, surrounded by junkie housemates in their shack. What a legacy for Errol Flynn . . .

One facet of a woman.

A different facet entirely.

Precious Amy.

CHAPTER 8

Back in New York

Nat Wartell of Crown Books had paid us a healthy advance. We split 50/50 minus charges Robin deducted for back rent on the New York studio and the Jamaican guest cottage. He suggested I hang around a few weeks longer and go over the galleys with him but did not offer me further use of the studio on 42nd.

I phoned an Australian girlfriend, Yvonne Dunleavy, and asked if I could stay with her for two or three weeks. During my dancing days, Yvonne and I had become friends in Hong Kong where she had worked for The Hong Kong Standard newspaper. She moved to New York ahead of me and was reporting for The National Enquirer. Embarrassed by 'lowering her standards', as she put it, she was reluctant to tell people where she worked. She did admit the money was good.

"I only have the pull-out sofa in the living room," she said, tossing her mane of glossy, dark hair. "You can sleep there but you'll have to pay rent. Manhattan rents are a killer."

"Sure thing," I replied, eyeing the uncomfortable-looking brown sofa. Her walk-up apartment was hot, noisy and sparsely furnished but at least it was centrally located.

A day or two later, I met up with Robin in his accountant's office where we sipped coffee from oversized mugs.

"I've definitely decided to write the hooker's story," Robin said.

"That's a deviation from your normal genre. Have you been trying the goods?" I asked sarcastically.

He smirked and sat his coffee down.

"Anyway, you're right. It's not my usual genre but my nose tells me it's gonna make a lot of money. Right, Jack?" He glanced at his accountant for back-up. "But I won't write it, I'll just package it. It needs a female writer. I don't suppose you know one, do you?"

I raised my eyebrows. "Well, it just so happens I do. But let me check first and get back to you."

"Junie Moon, you're always full of surprises."

"Yeah, aren't I?"

A week later, I introduced Yvonne to Robin. Yvonne always looked classy and Robin's eyes lit up but Yvonne was having none of it. Nevertheless, she was anxious to quit The National Enquirer. For a substantial price, she was ready to work with Robin. Stupid me, I didn't think to ask for a finder's fee and still I paid rent.

Robin invited me to lunch at The Four Seasons. I guessed it was a 'thank you' for putting him together with Yvonne.

"How's it going Robin?" I asked as the waiter seated me.

"Yvonne is a godsend," he replied. "Thanks for introducing us."

"She's a clever girl. How is she getting on with Zaviera?"

"No problems. The book is moving fast. I just love you Aussie women." He set his martini down, looked thoughtful, then asked, "Would you like to meet Zaviera before you leave?"

"I knew a few hookers in Hong Kong. They weren't exactly scintillating company."

"Ha! Don't underestimate Zaviera. She's one tough Dutch cookie. That's one hooker I'm going to make very, very happy." He paused. "Hell! There you have it! The title . . . I'll call it 'The Happy Hooker'."

"With a title like that, I'm sure you will have a bestseller," I sniffed. "And if The Khaki Mafia doesn't make me a rich woman also, I just might be damned mad."

"Junie Moon, sex is the hot market right now." He sipped his drink, adding, "So do you want to meet her or not?"

"Well, I've recently met Rusty Calley of 'The My Lai Massacre' and Sonny Grasso of 'The French Connection'. Why not a whore?"

It was an inauspicious meeting. Zaviera bristled the moment I entered her apartment. Maybe my body language was arrogant. She pretty much ignored me as she gushed over Robin. I was surprised by the cheapness of the apartment. Except for the obligatory mirrors, it was nothing like the plush, erotic whorehouse I was expecting. The madam was equally underwhelming and I could not believe that she or her place of business attracted high level 'johns'. Still, I did not doubt that Robin's upcoming book could elevate her into history. He often commented that one of his assets was a good commercial nose. Whenever I mentioned talented writers whose work I enjoyed, he always retorted, "There are plenty of authors writing beautiful words but they have nothing to say. I pass them every day on my way to the bank."

I looked at Zaviera's half-exposed, drooping breasts. Breast implants had recently become available in the U.S. after great success in Japan. Before I left the Land of the Rising Sun, I witnessed thousands of flat-chested dance hostesses lining up to get them. Dow Chemicals had made a fortune exporting silicone to Japan.

I wondered why Zaviera had not seized upon the business opportunity of making an investment in her sagging inventory. Her narrow face, framed by lank, oily hair, looked sallow and unhealthy. I remember thinking that she would benefit from a shampoo. I know! I know! . . . . meow, meow!

Her boyfriend, whom she referred to as The Silver Fox, was personable and rather attractive with a thick head of—yes—silver hair. He seemed devoted to her and I concluded she must possess a basketful of tricks surpassing those of the Kama Sutra.

FOOTNOTE:

'The Happy Hooker' did outsell 'The Khaki Mafia' by a landslide. Zaviera, Yvonne and Robin did all pass me as they ran to the bank. And, yes, I *was* jealous as hell! And *why* did I not ask for that finder's fee . . .

CHAPTER 9

Australia's Outback

During the year it had taken our book to hit the bookshelves, I tread water. Still feeling a bit rudderless, I had come no closer to adopting a child.

After leaving New York, I had gone immediately to my family's dairy farm in Australia. I loved my family dearly yet, even with them, I did not 'fit in'. My siblings, now grown, had little in common with me other than parentage. Indeed, my mother, when referring to me, often lamented, "I'm sure the hospital gave me the wrong baby." Was she joking? Another of her frequent comments: "After June visits, I feel as if a cyclone has blown through."

I sometimes wondered if I was on the wrong track. My family members were all so stable, striving in 'respectable' jobs to attain that nice home, that secure retirement. I had always been able to make money but it meant little to me as I lived for each day. Whenever I doubted myself and my lifestyle, I clung to the words of Oscar Wilde: "*To live is the rarest thing in the world. Most people exist; that is all!*" Yet it did make me an outcast, if only in my own mind. But it was certainly preferable to boredom.

After visiting the family for a couple of weeks, I had chuffed alone around Australia's outback on a motor bike. Passing through some of the small provincial towns on my way north, I had been refused service in a few cafés. I suppose my mode of dress made the proprietors' nervous. It was a time when women uniformly encased their legs in nylon stockings and wore knee-length dresses, or skirts and blouses. For practicality, I had unearthed my old Vietnam army fatigues and boots. And maybe it wasn't just the army gear but the rifle slung across my back that they objected to. Yet I was not heading into 'snake country' unarmed.

In Alice Springs, the heart of the Outback, a family had climbed from their late model BMW and taken offense when they saw me sitting on the gutter kerb, talking to a bunch of aboriginals. I ignored their rude comments but it gave me food for thought. Amid high-society in New York, I had felt like a Martian and, here in the Australian outback, I apparently still didn't fit in. For the hundredth time since leaving Vietnam, I wondered just where I did belong.

Nevertheless, I enjoyed the natural beauty of the desert with its craggy canyons and monolithic rocks. It was the dry season and I camped beneath the brilliant stars at night with nothing between me and Mother Earth except a vinyl ground sheet. At Ayers Rock, huge flocks of white, sulphur-crested cockatoo's routinely woke me at dawn as they left on their daily sojourns, screeching and blotting out the sky while passing overhead in a seemingly endless procession. The flapping of a million wings and the barrage of piercing calls were more effective than any alarm clock. As their noise receded, the pink sky was gradually revealed. I then rose, brushed a feather or two from my hair, and lit the fire. There is nothing better than starting a new day with a cup of hot tea in cold, desert air.

Other hardy campers were sprinkled around the base of Ayers Rock. We shared our food, our drinks, and our stories. They came from all over the world—everywhere but Australia that is. The Aussies were all away exploring England. I remember a handful of Japanese tourists who were grateful for my inept translations. I recall a young Scotsman who entertained us around the huge bonfire each night with his bagpipes. Such pleasures cost nothing.

They were, of course, the days before 'civilization' arrived. The days before the government, observing 'political correctness' and trying to appease the aboriginals, changed the name of Ayers Rock to the aboriginal word, Uluru. The days before a hotel was erected for less hardy tourists. The days before restrictions about climbing the rock were implemented.

That wonderful, wild outback was more healing than any high-paid psychiatrist. But, too soon, my feet grew itchy as they invariably did. I stashed my fatigues, gave away my camping gear and headed for Europe.

Stopping off in London, I forked over a chunk of my book advance to a matchmaker who promised to set me up with a millionaire. After all, if I *must* marry to adopt that child, it may as well be to a rich man.

Unfortunately, the millionaire and I had busy schedules and the only time we could catch up was in between flights at Charles De Gaulle airport when we were both heading elsewhere.

I found my way to the meeting place. He was already at the restaurant, wearing an identifying red handkerchief in his breast pocket. As I approached, he stood and held out a chair, his eyes appraising me from head to toe. He was tall and only slightly overweight. I was relieved that he seemed quite normal and pleased that he didn't smoke. The lunch went well. We talked a lot, drank a little and found a few things we had in common. He was average looking and pleasant; I could probably put up with him. Of course, I did not immediately pop the question about adopting a street orphan. As we prepared to continue on our separate journeys, I pulled out a pen, ready to jot down the place and date of our next rendezvous.

"I've enjoyed meeting you," he said, stooping to hug me. "You are one smart, attractive lady. But we won't meet again. You're too short."

Pulling myself up to my full five-feet three inches, I retorted, "Wouldn't it be more gentlemanly to concede you are too tall?"

In Europe, I adopted a more conventional lifestyle. I was living on The Hotel Schiff (a stationary vessel anchored permanently on the Rhine River in Frankfurt) when Robin contacted me.

"It's time to return, Junie Moon," his voice crackled over the phone in the ship's overcrowded office. I was leaning uncomfortably across the desk, stretching the coiled cord to bring the phone as close to my ear as possible. "Nat has set up a full schedule of radio and television interviews for us."

I digested the timely news. Winter was coming and Frankfurt had been smothering under heavy fog the last few mornings. Besides, I was sick and tired of eating hard-boiled eggs and cold bread rolls for breakfast. There seemed to be nothing else on the ship's menu and, if there was, my Deutsche was too limited to order it.

Arriving back in the U.S., I discovered 'The Khaki Mafia' was selling in the hundreds of thousands but not in the millions

I had hoped for. It hit the 'Best Seller' list in Robin's hometown of Boston but not nationally.

During my absence, Robin and Liz had divorced and the 'Witch' had disappeared as well. Liz kept the New York condo and Robin had acquired a country estate in nearby Westport, Connecticut. Remaking his image, he had added leather-patched tweed jackets to his Brooks Brothers wardrobe, purchased a limousine and hired Vincent, a cheerful Jamaican, who now doubled as Robin's live-in chauffer/houseman.

I accepted Robin's invitation of temporary accommodation at the Westport estate. He and I did the promotional tour, accompanied by Lisa, Crown Publisher's P.R. woman. In New York and L.A., we were guests on most major television talk programs. There was Mike Douglas and David Frost and Merv Griffin and shows like "Whose Line Is It" amongst others since forgotten. We sometimes woke at daybreak and raced to have breakfast with the truck drivers. These were the men who placed the books in the book stores. If they liked you, they placed your books at eye level.

Accompanied by Lisa, who took good care of us, we flew to a different city each day, hitting all the major cities on the east coast and in the midwest. We gave newspaper, magazine and radio interviews and returned to the hotel in time for dinner each night. Once again, I reigned as Queen for a Day.

With Liz out of the picture, Robin was again in hot pursuit. His new lifestyle was alluring. I enjoyed Westport and his acreage property with its picturesque gardens. As I contemplated a life spent between there and Port Antonio, I was tempted. But I knew I could never be happy in an 'open marriage' and I saw no other options with Robin's infidelity.

Visiting at the family farm in Australia.

CHAPTER 10

High Society ... Again

Growing up at the mercy of fate, I experienced both wealth and poverty. Maybe that was why I consistently avoided 'the middle of the road'. For me it was either 'five stars' or slumming.

My mother was a superb seamstress and throughout even the poorest years, we were always well dressed.

"Remember, June," she used to say, "first appearances stick. Always stand straight, sit with your legs together, speak correctly and dress well. Nan dresses beautifully. Everyone admires her."

"But Nan is rich," I had argued.

"You don't have to be rich to have style," Mum countered, pulling on a rubber dairy boot. "Coordinate colors. Wear what suits you, not what you see in the magazines."

I smiled as she bustled away to milk the cows. She was wearing her customary overalls and a battered straw hat. But if she went into town to buy a few groceries, she would be most properly attired.

Taking after my grandmother, I always found great pleasure in clothes. In Vietnam, I had, out of practicality, worn fatigues. Now with money in my pocket once more, I was running amok amid the shops of Manhattan. My mini-skirts and boots were disappearing. Indeed, the previous week, my full-length photo had made the front page of the prestigious Women's Wear Daily. Forsaking glamour for elegance, I was pictured wearing a slim, floor-length emerald green and navy tartan skirt topped by a double-breasted velvet blazer.

Again I was on the fringes of 'the social set' but this time I found it enjoyable. At one of those New York cocktail parties, I shared a dream with Ed McMahon, Johnny Carson's sidekick.

"I'm going to have a Chinese junk built one day," I said. Detecting his interest, I elaborated. "In Hong Kong, I went aboard several. They have wider beams than a regular vessel, making them really spacious and I'm told they are seaworthy."

"Really?"

"Yes. I will hire a Chinese family as crew and take a bunch of Asian orphans and cruise the world. We will become international citizens."

"It's a nice dream," he said and he must have meant it because a short while later I learned he bought a Chinese junk but he did not fill it with orphans.

The book promotion was over. While In Australia, I had discovered that foreign adoptions were totally impossible in that country, so I had no intention of returning home. I decided to investigate Florida with a view to buying a home in that warm climate. Home ownership was the first step towards adopting the child. Simultaneously, I needed to find a suitable marriage mate so the adoption agencies would consider me. It was time to leave Westport but still I lingered.

Propinquity had fostered an undeniable affection between me and Robin. I admired so much about him; his love of country, his courage, his easy going nature, his quick mind. While writing The Khaki Mafia, our mutual love of the young fighting men had drawn us together. The previous week, at Robin's instigation, we had traveled to Fort Bragg and held a party for several Green Beret friends, handing out copies of our book.

I was well aware of Robin's shortcomings but God knows I wasn't faultless. We fell into a pattern of unorthodox domesticity. Somewhere along the way, after sharing an evening of alcohol-stoked reminiscences, I had fallen into his bed. There were no fireworks. Robin's tepid passion reached its performance peak when he emitted a gasp. Or so I thought, until realizing it was a snort; an indication that he had fallen asleep on top of me.

The next morning, neither one of us referred to the previous night's event. I wondered was he even aware of it. I thought of the pleasant lifestyle he led. The quaint town of Westport, only an hour's drive from Manhattan, afforded the perfect mix of country tranquility and city indulgences.

Robin's house had previously belonged to the artist Steve Dohanos (famous for all those Saturday Evening Post covers). The wide hallway doubled as an art gallery, with sun and sky visible through the glass ceiling. The cedar walls and wood-burning fireplaces kept a perpetually pleasing fragrance in the air. It was all just too comforting. I loved the green hills with their white railing fences. I loved the country lanes with their canopies of pink flowering dogwood trees. I loved the sprinkling of beautiful farm houses and the cultured people who lived in them. And then there was Vincent. Always at our beck and call; always cheerful, respectful but never servile. Maybe I could settle down and live very happily with Robin.

I shook the daydreams from my head. Despite the inadequacies of our first coupling, Robin and I had continued the physical side of our relationship. For me, sex began in the brain and Robin was always immensely stimulating, therefore, desirable. I didn't need porno movies or sex magazines to turn me on. My idea of a good sex scene was in the movie 'From Here to Eternity' when Burt Lancaster and Deborah Kerr lay, kissing in the ocean. Or, later still, in a scene from 'Out Of Africa' when Robert Redford shampooed Meryl Streep's hair. This was not a streak of puritanism. I was uninspired by the most acrobatic sexual acts unless they were coupled with emotional desire. I had attended one of Zaviera's parties and left early, feeling no desire to participate.

That said, our sexual incompatibility did occasionally trouble me. How long would it be before one of us strayed? He had a history of perpetual infidelity, an enigma to me after I became aware of how adversely his drinking affected his lovemaking.

And how about adopting children? Robin referred to all kids as rug rats. He would run a mile at such a suggestion. I knew him too well. He loved controversy, loved sensationalism. I believed it was all a huge cover, a camouflage really, for the genuinely conservative person he actually was. I had noticed him cringe if I wore something that he considered too revealing. Yet it was my audacious, nonconforming attitude that fascinated him; eventually he would tire of that.

"I have great news!" Robin burst into the study, his coat dusted in snow, his cheeks flushed. He and Vincent had just returned from town. I felt a warm buzz of pleasure that he was home. Bustling over to the fireplace, he warmed his hands before the blaze. Vincent followed him into the room saying, "I'll make dinner now, Mr. Moore. Maybe forty minutes. You want a cocktail first?"

Robin shrugged his coat off. "Don't ask dumb questions!"

Vincent grinned and strode to the cocktail cabinet. "You, too, Miss June?" he tossed over his shoulder.

"No thanks, Vincent. I still have one. I'll wait for dinner."

"Don't you want to hear my news, Junie Moon?" Robin teased.

"If it's good, out with it."

"'The Khaki Mafia' is going to be made into a movie."

"Wow," I yelled, jumping up and dropping my book. "Tell me more."

"Hannah Weinstein will produce it. She is well-respected and the investor is Edgar Bronfman, the owner of Seagram's whisky."

"That's terrific!"

"She's anxious to meet you," Robin continued. "I told her I would bring you into the city tomorrow."

"I'm so excited." I bustled towards him and tried to pull him into a little dance. He smiled as he withdrew from my arms.

"Why don't you wear your new mink coat? The weather is miserable," he said.

I did wear the coat; my first fur. Hannah, small and middle-aged, was more conservative in a brown gabardine trench coat. Nevertheless, the meeting went well and we quickly established a good rapport. Over the following weeks, we spoke frequently and things progressed well.

Then, one day, she asked me to join her at The Four Seasons Hotel. We lunched with Ann Margret and her agent, Alan Carr. It looked promising that Ann Margret would be playing me in the movie and she wanted to get to know me.

To my surprise, she was totally unlike her sexy screen image. She was quiet and almost shy, not the least bit arrogant. When she told us her husband Roger was at home sick, her voice was so openly filled with love and tenderness that I, a cynic regarding marriage, experienced a little jab of envy.

Not easily impressed by people, I found myself a little tongue-tied. She was so beautiful; it was difficult not to stare. Her flawless, pale skin was as smooth as alabaster and her eyes could melt any heart.

I, the only passenger, was sitting up front in a C130 Hercules Transport. The cavity of the enormous cargo carrier was unlit and dim. We lurched occasionally, at the mercy of wind turbulence, and I felt my stress levels rising. The plane bounced and when the cargo moved slightly, I shivered. Despite my best efforts to ignore the dim shapes in the poor, late afternoon light, my eyes seemed to be drawn there and I regretted hitching a ride on this particular plane. However, I had become desperate after waiting in the dust for hours. Nightfall had approached and I needed to get home.

The plane dropped sharply again and the cargo moved once more, as if in protest to the rough ride. My hands began to sweat and a sea of young men's faces swam before my eyes. Anguished faces! Dead faces! Faces belonging to the young men riding inside those dark, plastic body bags, their voices forever quieted. Thump, thump, thump . . . my heart exploded in my ears. I wanted to run and unzip the bags, setting the men free. But I couldn't move; I was too scared. When one body bag rolled towards me, I screamed.

"Wake up, Junie Moon." Robin was shaking me. I stared at him, unseeing for a few moments while hyperventilating.

"You're having a nightmare," he said kindly.

My breathing started to calm. "I thought they had finished," I murmured, shaken. "I can't sleep again, Robin. Do you mind if I pour myself a brandy?"

The following morning, everything was beautiful again. I glanced out the window and saw it was still snowing. The countryside looked like a Christmas card. Robin sat across from me as we ate a light breakfast before being driven into Manhattan by Vincent.

"You might need to see someone about your nightmares," Robin said between mouthfuls of toast.

"No. I rarely get them now. I'm sorry I woke you."

"I thought they had stopped."

"Not altogether."

"Ghosts, Junie Moon. Ghosts. Let them sleep."

Robin changed the subject. "Tell me again, what will you be doing in town today?"

"I have to meet Hannah Weinstein."

"Does she need me?"

"She didn't say so." I reached for the vegemite and spread some on my toast. Robin looked and grimaced.

"How can you eat that axle grease?" Pointedly, he reached for his vitamins, apparently appalled by my gastronomic choices.

"Hannah wants me to meet Jules later this afternoon."

"Jules Dassin, the director?" Robin frowned.

"Yeah! He flew in from Athens last night. They're dragging me off to Hawaii soon while they hash out the script with Stirling Silliphant."

"Damn it." Robin scowled. "Hannah is leaving me out of the loop. I was ignored last week when Ann Margret came into town." He stood abruptly. "Be ready to leave in ten minutes. I've got an appointment with my accountant this morning."

Throughout the hour-long trip, Robin buried his nose in The Wall Street Journal. He was seldom in such a grumpy mood; Hannah had offended him.

The previous week, when I had attended a small dinner gathering at her apartment, I realized that she wasn't particularly fond of Robin. She had rather brusquely told me that, now the book was written, he was no longer needed. At the time, I wondered was it a Jew versus Wasp thing but, as the dinner progressed, I realized that was not the case.

Hannah's overstuffed apartment was full of old-fashioned furniture and well-read books. The only other dinner guests were her close friends: the aging actress, Lillian Gish; and Leonard Bernstein, whom she affectionately called Lennie.

Frankly, although impressed, I was a little bored as they reminisced about old times. They graciously tried to include me in the conversation, asking about my Vietnam experiences. But, despite their best efforts, that old 'fish out of water' was still gasping for air.

While listening to the dinner conversation, I began to see how Hannah and Robin were worlds apart in so many ways. When I hesitantly told her of my adoption plans, she was excited and encouraging whereas Robin had been scornful. I guess motherhood just never fit the image he had of me.

Hannah told stories about her early days when, as a widow with young children, she had broken into the—at that time— man's world of movie producing. Maybe that's what linked us; we had both survived in a man's world. Although she did it on a much larger scale than I did.

Her movie-producing days began during a period when the entire film industry was the domain of 'whites' only. Apart from Sidney Poitier, there were few parts for black actors other than 'walk on' roles as slaves or servants. Not only actors but crews, grips, cameramen; all were white. Hannah broke the color barrier by employing and training Negros, as black American's were called back then.

I continued thinking of Hannah as Robin ignored me throughout the ride, hiding behind his paper. Maybe that liberal racial outlook was the link between Hannah and Stirling Silliphant. He had written the script for the first successful black movie, 'Shaft'.

Robin finally folded his paper and laid it on the opposite seat. "You might take the train back tonight," he mumbled. "You can grab a cab at the station. I'm going to have dinner with my attorney."

The night before I left for Hawaii, Robin didn't come home. It was the first time he had stayed away all night. I barely slept, listening to every sound, hoping it was the car. It was a windy night and an unlatched garden gate kept slamming. I jumped up repeatedly. The next morning, hoping against hope, I crept into his bedroom. The bed had not been slept in. My heart pounded and my hands shook. I tried to focus on the imminent trip but the joy seemed lost. Robin never displayed anger. Maybe he was getting revenge over not being invited to Hawaii. Or maybe he and I had just run our course.

I finished packing and lifted my bag off the bed. Despite our intimacy, Robin and I did not share a bedroom. Despondently, I hung the last of my winter clothes beside my mink coat in the closet. Just as I closed the closet door, I heard the car pull into the driveway. Hauling my suitcase to the living room, I tried to maintain my composure.

"Good morning, Robin." I greeted him with forced cheerfulness as he slunk in, red-eyed. He avoided looking at me but spotted the suitcase.

"You're going today, are you?"

"Had you forgotten?" With an effort, I kept my voice even.

"Of course not, Junie Moon. I let Vincent have the night off so I slept at my club." I knew he was referring to The New York Athletic Club, another prestige hangout for old, Wasp men. Although he frequented it often, during our time together, he had never slept there.

"No need to explain." I refused to go all hysterical as I had so often seen Liz do. "But I wonder, could you spare Vincent to drive me to the airport?"

"What? Hannah's not sending you a car?"

"I never asked."

"Well, okay. I'm planning on writing today so I don't need him."

I felt like beating him over the head but I made myself walk over and kiss him on the cheek. He smelled of stale whisky.

"Don't do anything I wouldn't do while I'm gone."

A dry imitation of a laugh escaped his throat. "That leaves me plenty of scope."

Two more passions; clothes and house decorating.

Telegraph

CITY FINAL

29th YEAR   PHONE 51-6811   BRISBANE, SATURDAY, JUNE 5, 1971   5 CENTS (AIR EXTRA)

EXCLUSIVE: Qantas chief says:

'POLICE KNEW ABOUT THE WHOLE AFFAIR'

From GRAHAM ECCLES

SYDNEY: "I still find it hard to believe that the police let 'Mr. Brown' get away." That is how Qantas general manager, Captain R. J. Ritchie summed up his feelings today about the $500,000 pay-off to the bomb hoaxer outside Qantas House in Sydney 11 days ago.

Captain Ritchie, the man who handed two blue suitcases crammed with half a million dollars to the hoaxer, expecting the police then to shadow him, said he still did not know what went wrong.

The police, he said, knew about the whole affair.

"When I went back up to my office and a senior police officer walked in a couple of minutes later and said, 'They've got a way.' I was absolutely dumbfounded," he told me "I still find the whole thing rather incredulous."

Captain Ritchie, 53, was speaking for the first time about his part in the great hoax story that has a nation wondering, as he does, how the police missed their man.

Captain Ritchie told me he knew positively that at least two shadow cars were waiting in Cutlery Square, outside Qantas House, when he handed over the ransom money to "Mr. Brown."

"What went wrong with the operation? Well, I guess that was all come out in the wash one day," he said.

Captain Ritchie outlined the role of those last nine vital minutes which followed "Mr. Brown's" 5.30 p.m. telephone call with the pay-off instructions.

"My assistant general manager Phil Howson, took the call as he had done each time Mr. Brown telephoned.

"After he had hung up, about 5.26 p.m., the police were told that the yellow Hertz van would pull up at the front door at 5.45 p.m. and three times, and the driver would wave his keys on the window.

"There were at least eight minutes after that for the police to do whatever they had in mind.

"There were about nine or 10 policemen — there included Commonwealth police — in either my office or the adjacent lounge, where they had a telephone line to the CIB.

"About 5.40 I mentioned generally, and to no one in particular, that it was time to go. I sat outside, and so are other Qantas executives, that a senior CIB detective was standing in the room when I said it."

HEADING FOR LIFTS

Captain Ritchie said he went out of his office to a large floor-to-ceiling safe where the money was being held. Police and staff were guarding the money.

"As I picked up the suitcase two policemen were heading for the lift," he continued. "It was mentioned that it might be better for them to take the lifts at the northern end of the building.

"They left at least 30 seconds before I walked down the corridor to a lift at the other end of the building."

Captain Ritchie said he had since learned that a senior CIB detective was telling the CIB operations room of the pay-off time and that he (Captain Ritchie) was about to make the pay-off.

"I cannot tell you now I know but that is right," he said.

Captain Ritchie said that when he remained to his office there was no policeman in sight. He telephoned the CIB and gave them a detailed description of the hoaxer and the pick-up van.

Captain Ritchie, denied that he had rushed out of his office at the ransom time without telling police he was going downstairs.

● CONTINUED, PAGE 17

INFLATION POINTS TO TOUGH BUDGET, P.3

A fashion spectacular

Today's Grand Pcall at Eagle Farm race course rivalled the glamour of the Melbourne Cup as Queensland's best-dressed women enthusiastically joined in our first fashion On The Turf competition. One of the early arrivals who gave an indication of the glamour to come was New York audience, Jane Collins, who chose a knitted...

CITY FORECAST: Fine, fine, min. near 51 deg. Sun tides: High, 7.45 a.m., 7.55 p.m.; low, 1.15 a.m., 1.22 p.m.

CHAPTER 11

Hawaii

I looked around my suite in the Kahala Hilton Hotel, my delight at being back in Hawaii somewhat subdued by the previous night's events. During my years in Vietnam, Hawaii had been my favorite R&R destination. This visit was the most exciting of all. A movie was being made about me!

I walked out onto the balcony and looked at the flawless blue sky, the sparkling ocean, and sighed with pleasure. The phone jangled. I pulled my eyes from Hilton Head and ran to answer.

"Meet us down at The Verandah restaurant in an hour," Hannah said.

"Right. I'll bring my photos of Vietnam. Jules said he wants to take a look at them."

Hannah had been friends with Jules for years, way back before he directed 'Around the World in 80 Days' for Mike Todd; way before he married the actress Melina Mercouri and Mike married Elizabeth Taylor. And way before he left the U.S. to escape the purge of Herbert Hoover, the head of the FBI who was so nutty as to see a communist around every corner, especially in Hollywood.

Changing into a pair of white slacks and a black-and-white striped T-shirt, I hoped to make a favorable impression on Stirling. His perceptions of me would influence the way he wrote me into the script.

The restaurant was half empty as I entered, most diners having already eaten. I spotted Jules and Hannah at a corner table. Hannah wore a simple grey linen, shirt-waister dress and Jules was leaning towards her, his shock of white hair flopping as he spoke. Hannah gave scant thought to her appearance but she possessed a definite aura and I noticed that male colleagues paid her great respect.

"Pull up a seat, June dear," she said. "Order something light and we can get down to business. Stirling will join us shortly."

We finished our late lunch and the waiter was clearing the table when Stirling strode in looking very Hollywood. His casual white shirt, open at the throat, exposed a triangle of deeply-bronzed chest. Slightly crumpled beige cotton pants were tucked into shiny, brown leather boots that were laced all the way up to the knee. Almost handsome, he was tall and exuded confidence.

After ordering green tea, he placed a clipboard and ballpoint on the table. Hannah fiddled with the chunky, black tape recorder and began the first of my interrogations. Countless questions followed with little progress.

"June. We want to know the 'real' you," she said.

"Yes," Jules agreed. "We know that you have courage but what is it that motivates you?"

"I don't know," I said, trying to hide my irritation. "In Vietnam, I learned that no man, or woman, knows just how much courage they have, or have not, until they are tested. Likewise, just how honest they are, or are not, until they are tempted. Temporarily, I failed in the honesty department but finally I came through. I never wavered on the courage. I don't know what makes me tick. It's up to you to define me."

Sensing my growing frustration, no one responded immediately.

"Others knew it was wrong and they kept quiet," Hannah finally insisted. "Just what impelled you to do something?"

"I guess no one wanted to lose the money, including me. I think they probably tried not to think about the downside of what was happening. I like the things money can provide as well as the next man. But—and this is a big but—it is not my God and I won't 'stop at nothing' to get it."

Stirling kept writing away and Hannah continued taping but they were obviously dissatisfied. I felt dense, unable to give them what they wanted. Frustrated, I blurted out, "Maybe there's nothing inside me . . . I don't know what you want."

Hannah clicked off the recorder. "I think we've done enough for today. We'll have another session tomorrow. Get a rest and clear your head now."

On my way down, I had noticed a piano bar. I needed a stiff drink . . . or two.

The following three days were more of the same and after such great anticipation, I felt like a failure, unable to please them. Since all my public exposure, I often felt that way; as if people were expecting much more from me than what I was able to give.

Footnote;

As I write this, once again I think of how times have changed. Today everyone is obsessed with celebrity. While I was garnering so much publicity—first from the newspaper headlines, then from the book—it never entered my mind to hire a public relations agent to optimize my exposure.

I look back in wonderment at the things I have done. And just occasionally, the words of Orson Scott Card (Enders Game) spring to mind.

'Perhaps it is impossible to wear an identity without becoming what you pretend to be.'

I remember being scared in Vietnam, yet still doing things that I did not have to do. In retrospect, I sometimes wonder what drove me.

Robin and I shared some tender moments.

CHAPTER 12

Goodbye Robin

I never thought I would be happy to say goodbye to Hawaii. However, my departure from Westport kept replaying in my mind and I was anxious to get back and resolve things with Robin.

Hannah let me out of the taxi at Penn station and I boarded the train for Westport where Vincent was waiting for me.

"Mr. Moore, he's in New York. He'll take the train home. I am picking him up at 6:30," he informed me while opening the car door. "Did you have a good trip?"

"So-so," I answered. "The sunshine was nice. I think it is time to head to Florida. I don't like winter."

We pulled into the driveway. "Mr. Moore told me to make a special nice dinner for you tonight. You wait for him."

I nodded, my heart thumping with hope as I stepped out into the cold. Shivering, I quickly followed Vincent inside. He set my luggage down in front of my closed bedroom door and left.

Opening the door, I stopped in my tracks, mouth agape. The bed, which I had left neatly made, was a mess. Why? Had there been house guests and, if so, why hadn't they used another bedroom? I strode to the bed and threw the blankets onto the floor. The sheets were really crumpled and held telltale stains. I felt a sense of dread. Surely Robin hadn't slept with someone in my bed? But, obviously, someone had. It must have been him but why not in his own bed? Why not in another guest room? My hands shook. This must be deliberate! I remembered the cruel psychological games he had played with Liz.

Painful, breathtaking jabs needled my heart. An angry red mist swirled in my head and I leaned against the bed post to steady myself. I always knew we didn't have the grand romance but I deserved better than this. And the unexpected intensity of my feelings only added to the shock. How was I going to handle the situation when he came home? No doubt, he would expect me to rant and rave like a mad woman the way Liz had. He seemed to thrive on such performances but I wouldn't give him that satisfaction. Going to the door, I called Vincent.

"Yes, Miss June?" He hurried into view.

"Who has been sleeping in my room? Why wasn't the bed made?"

"I don't know, Miss June. The door was shut. I did not know. I'll make the bed now."

"Thanks. Get clean sheets will you?" I didn't quite believe him but it wasn't his fault.

While I waited for Vincent to return, I opened the closet door. This time, my mouth fell to the floor. My winter clothes were hanging there but my new mink coat was gone. Unable to believe my eyes, I pawed through my dresses, hoping to find the coat pushed to the back. No! I ran into Robin's room and looked in his closet. There was no sign of it. I felt like crying. It was my first fur coat; an extravagant purchase. Then I remembered

Robin's ex-girlfriend, the 'Witch'. He had never shown much discretion with the women he bedded. As long as they clung to his every word with bated breath, he would bed anyone. That didn't say much for me.

It was going to be a hard evening to get through. Why was he even planning to dine with me if he had found someone else and was so blatant about it? At that moment, I realized with surprise that I must have cared for him far more than I ever acknowledged. Otherwise, why was my brain reeling and my chest so tight? But I would never hang around and become a victim of his games the way Liz had. Our book collaboration would demand a tie of sorts for the immediate future but it was time to say goodbye.

CHAPTER 13

Florida

I constantly refer to the never-ending effect of fate. My move to Florida was no exception.

Fortunately, Robin and I had parted in a civilized manner. In fact, he had been really nice . . . Remorseful? Guilty? Glad to be rid of me? Whatever, he had phoned The Jockey Club in Miami, a private club of which he was a member, and booked me in as his guest. I was grateful because I needed a base from which to look around and find a house. Nevertheless, I was still angry but it was the hurt that shocked me. Love must have crept up on me insidiously. In Vietnam, I had learned to steel myself and turn away from love. I hoped I hadn't forgotten how.

I looked unseeingly out the window of the American Airlines plane while waiting for take-off.

"I think you are in my seat," a deep, masculine voice interrupted my thoughts. It sounded familiar. Startled, I looked up.

"Good heavens, Leon! I haven't seen you in ages." My thoughts raced, pulling up the past. "Where are you going? And, no! I haven't got your seat."

The big man laughed, displaying expensively-perfected teeth. "To Miami. That's where this plane is headed, isn't it?" He stowed his luggage overhead then dropped into the seat beside me.

"Brooke and I moved there a few months ago. How about you?"

"I'm relocating there, too."

"What a coincidence. You'll have to come out to Hallandale and visit us. Brooke will be so pleased to see you. She still knows no one in Florida."

I wasn't convinced Brooke, another Aussie, would be so pleased.

"What happened to your lovely resort in the Poconos?"

"It's sold. Brook hated the winters and it wasn't the best environment for raising Glen. The guests kept spoiling him, feeding him candy and junk when we weren't looking."

I recalled meeting Leon soon after returning from Jamaica. At that time, I was dating Peter Davis, a restaurateur who owned a trendy little Manhattan place called The Jamaican Arms. Leon, a frequent lunch customer, became friendly with Peter and we often sat with him. He always ate alone so we had never met his wife. As the friendship between Peter and Leon grew, Leon invited the two of us to spend a weekend at the resort as his guests.

Peter, like most New Yorkers, did not own a car. Leon generously offered to send a limousine from the resort's fleet to transport us. All that week, I had looked forward to a weekend in the country, delighted to be taking a break from Yvonne's hot, noisy apartment with the uncomfortable sofa bed.

During the trip, I lounged in the back seat of the limo as we sped over ninety miles of asphalt. Peter dozed beside me and

I idly wondered what Leon's wife would be like, assuming she would be Jewish the same as him.

Upon arrival, we had entered the resort's cavernous, main building and I remembered well the smell of cedar timber walls. Logs crackled as they burned in an open fireplace. The receptionist paged Leon who soon arrived with his blonde, blue-eyed, two-year-old son in tow.

"Welcome," he said, shaking Peter's hand before giving me a hug. "This is our son, Glen. Did I mention my wife is Australian?"

"Australian? Why didn't you say so sooner? Now I'm doubly pleased we came."

"Brooke and I met on a plane flying out of Tokyo," Leon elaborated. "She worked there in the Australian Embassy."

"Two Aussie women. Wow, that will surely keep us on our toes." Peter grinned.

"I told her you are Australian and she's anxious to meet you."

Leon had been guiding us outdoors as we talked and I recalled inhaling the fresh mountain air while crossing a wide deck overlooking a lake. Spotting three people chatting with their backs towards us, Leon called out, "Brooke. Honey, have you got a minute? Come meet my friends."

The tallest one, a blonde woman, turned. My eyes widened in shock. Worked in The Australian Embassy, be damned! She and I had been strippers in some of Japan's top nightclubs.

Her face registered horror. Limply extending her hand, she coldly muttered, "Pleased to meet you."

Taking my cue from her, I played the charade and shook hands.

"It was love at first sight," Leon babbled, unaware of any tension. "By the time our plane touched down, I had asked her to marry me."

"That was fast," Peter said.

"Too fast for my family, especially with Brooke being a shiksa."

"What's that?" I asked.

"A non-Jewish woman." Leon laughed. "You see I'm not a very good Jew."

"Well, I can see why you fell for her," Peter responded gallantly. Indeed, Brooke was a beautiful, classy woman whom I remembered as being smart and ambitious. We had never been friends. She remained aloof from other strippers and was neither popular nor fun. I, on the other hand, was the ringleader of devilry.

"Her only failing," Leon said, his eyes twinkling, "is that, with her clerical background, I can't get her to do any of my typing."

I remembered the difficulty I had in repressing a snicker.

"We hire people for that," Brooke snootily replied. "Isn't it enough to be a mother and run this place, too?"

During the ensuing weekend, Brooke avoided me. When I finally caught her alone, she whispered, "Thanks for not giving me away. The truth would devastate Leon."

I gave my promise but she remained clearly uncomfortable in my presence.

After I left New York for Australia and Europe, I lost track of them. But now, fate was bringing Brooke and me together for a third time. I thought of that line from Casablanca: "Of all the gin joints in . . ." Only I substituted it with, "Of all the airplanes in . . ."

The plane was about to land. Leon gave me his phone number and I told him I could be found at the Jockey Club.

"That's a little highbrow." He said. "Anyway, Brooke will be waiting at the airport. You'll have to say hullo."

I was wearing a revealing blouse. Leon looked pointedly at my plunging neckline; not for the first time, I noted. "You can't close your top with a pin before meeting Brooke, can you?"

I spluttered with restrained laughter.

CHAPTER 14

Some Ladies Dine Alone

At the Jockey Club, I spent most mornings reading the real estate section of The Miami Herald while sunbathing by the pool. There were no other lone, young women at the exclusive club so I attracted attention. I was never short of a partner for an afternoon game of backgammon, the craze back then.

Although young ladies rarely traveled alone—this was before the advent of female business executives—I was always comfortable with my own company. I had mastered a few tricks to avoid pests, pity or disrespect. I walked purposefully, always carried a book or camera and avoided most eye contact. When eating out in restaurants, I refused to be seated in a corner by the kitchen or ignored by the staff, treatment customarily reserved for lone female travelers. I was never intimidated into ordering room service as many women did.

Dinner theaters or clubs with floorshows were my favorite evening venues. When phoning ahead for a reservation, the first query was always, "For how many ma'am?" After I replied "one", the voice at the other end almost always lost respect. Mustering my haughtiest tone, I then insisted on a table with a good view of the show. I next requested they read the wine list to me. After selecting a fine red, I demanded they uncork the bottle and let it breathe prior to my arrival. I always tipped well and having set the scene, I returned to the same places repeatedly. Naturally, I was remembered and assured of the royal treatment. On one occasion, I was mistakenly addressed as Lady Collins and felt no need to make the correction.

Such were the times and the lengths we women had to go to travel the world alone. Today, lone female diners are commonplace and they can avoid unwelcome attention by opening their laptop or gluing their iPhone to their ear.

During my first week in Miami, I inspected numerous homes from Coral Gables to Fort Lauderdale. Nice homes but all boringly similar. Surely, becoming a mother did not require I purchase the typical white-picket fenced house in suburbia? It was enough that I must marry.

Expanding my search for something more exotic, I finally found what I wanted. Not a house but a boat! And not just any boat but one with history; it had featured prominently in the James Bond movie, 'Thunderball.'

"Is this vessel suitable as a live-aboard?" I asked the boat owner over the phone.

"Bettcha bottom dollar, lady," said the man in a rough voice, indicating an excessive use of cigarettes.

"When can I see it?"

"I'm sorry. I have to work during the day. You'll have to wait until Sunday. Other buyers are looking at it on Saturday."

His suggestion of urgency did not squelch any warning voice, such was my excitement.

"Okay. How about tonight?"

He eagerly agreed.

That evening, I was planning to meet some acquaintances in a nightclub. My tan looked fabulous against the lime-green dress and my hair hung long and blonde down my bare back. Encircling my wrist was a wide, 18-karat gold Chinese bracelet set with large Alexandrite stones.

Climbing into The Jockey Club's limousine, I handed the driver a slip of paper.

"If you can wait for me at the first address, I won't be long, Charles. Then we can continue on to the club." He turned on the overhead light and frowned as he read the slip of paper.

"If you don't mind me saying, Ma'am, this address is in a bad part of town."

"Well, of course. Not everyone can keep their boat in the heart of the city."

"Many do," he answered stonily, putting the vehicle into gear before pulling out onto Biscayne Boulevard.

After a few wrong turns and some backtracking, Charles at last found the marina. It was difficult to read the shabby sign in the poor lighting. This was nothing like the well-lit docks around the Jockey Club. There were no stately, large vessels rocking at anchor here. I looked at the long, narrow dock which disappeared over the dark water into nothingness.

"Are you sure you'll be alright, Ma'am?" He had not turned off the engine.

"I'm okay," I replied, stemming any misgivings. Charles shrugged, opened my door, then quickly jumped back inside the vehicle. I heard the door locks click into place.

There wasn't a soul anywhere as I traipsed warily along the unlit rickety dock. The few boats I passed appeared decrepit. Feeling uneasy, I thought of turning back. A singular light shone beacon-like from a pole in the distance. I increased my pace and, within seconds, the high heel of one of my shoes caught in a crack between the planks.

"Damn it" I cussed, bending to set it free. Was that a warning to abort this mission? Still, I teetered on a few more steps and suddenly, like an apparition, she loomed up out of the night, all white and magnificent and majestic. I gazed at the two dinghies hanging from davits on the upper deck and exhaled excitedly. This beauty was as out of place on the shabby dock as I was.

"It's a little beauty, ain't it?" The voice from the dark made me jump. He emerged into the circle of yellow light, a cigarette dangling from his lower lip as if glued there.

"Are you sure this is the boat from the movie?" I asked sceptically.

"Sure. Take a look." He handed over a sheaf of slightly cracked black-and-white, ten-by-eight glossies. It certainly looked like her . . . from the back.

"What happened to her bow?" I asked, stepping forward and noting the flat surface where the pointed bow should have been. This was not the same image as in the photos.

Ungluing his cigarette, he threw it into the water. "Well, it's like this. Didya see the movie 'Thunderball'?"

"Yes, I did."

"Then ya must remember the scene at the end where there was a big explosion and they sped away, leavin' the back half of the boat burnin' in the water."

"What?" I wasn't following.

"That's all movie magic. Ya see there were actually two vessels joined together. The front part they escaped in was a hydrofoil. This back half has no engine. It was attached behind the hydrofoil which towed it and could jettison it off. You might say it is a floatin' home designed to look like a ship."

"Like half a ship, you mean. I'm looking for a live-aboard but it would be nice if it had a front end and an engine. Where is the hydrofoil half now?"

"In Russia. I might be able to put ya in touch with the owner if ya serious."

"I am. Please turn her lights on so I can go aboard."

"I'm sorry, lady. The generator batteries need chargin' but I have a flashlight. Follow me."

I stepped back. "No! I will inspect her in daylight."

"I'm showin' her to someone else tomorrow."

I knew this beauty was just the image I craved and I couldn't let her escape. Don't ask me why, but all thoughts of homeless orphans were forgotten. I was thinking 'party time' again.

The next day, after I concluded the deal, I was so excited that I had to share the good news with someone. I phoned Robin but he didn't answer. Then I thought of Leon. He loved boats and, when I told him, he seemed to share my excitement.

"Call me when you're moving aboard," he said. "I'll have Brooke pack a picnic lunch and we'll come down and help you celebrate your boat-warming."

Two days later, they arrived in their big, blue Cadillac loaded with picnic hampers. After we parked, with Glen skipping along the dock beside us, Leon commented on the poor condition of the entire marina.

"Yeah. I think the seller was down on his luck. This was probably all he could afford."

The vessel loomed into view and I frowned. She did not look as grand as I remembered. Drawing closer, I could even see a few rust spots. Alarm bells began belatedly clanging. Could this be the same wonderful vision I'd seen previously? The only part that looked grand right now were the two dinghies hanging from the top deck davits.

"Maybe she just needs a fresh coat of paint," I said hopefully as we stepped aboard.

Brooke and I stumbled around, holding Glen's hands while looking for a place to sit and have our picnic. Leon inspected the vessel, poking into all the corners, peering into cavities below deck and trying the steps to the upper deck.

"I don't like the look of her," he said ominously. "I think you've been hoodwinked."

"Shall I get the food out?" Brooke tried to lighten the pronouncement.

"Hell no! I think this piece of shit is likely to sink. Let's get back on dry land."

I was devastated. How could I have been so stupid? I didn't do drugs so I had no excuse. Was I such a sucker? Some years back, a trusted friend had robbed me of a huge haul of jewelry and now this. Would I ever learn not to be impetuous? I was ashamed for Leon and Brooke to bear witness to my stupidity.

Leon interrupted my mental flagellation. "You can't stay here, June. It's not safe. You will have to come home and stay with us until you find somewhere else to live. Won't she, Brooke?"

Brooke half-heartedly agreed.

It was fortunate that I accepted the invitation. The next day, my dream boat sank. She was declared a waterway hazard and the city made me pay to have her dredged up and salvaged.

CHAPTER 15

The Movie Deal Collapses

Hannah phoned me. The movie deal had fallen through. I couldn't believe it. Edgar Bronfman had already invested the first half a million dollars. What would make him pull out? It was such a blow. I tried to hide my intense disappointment. There was the loss of money and I had been so thrilled by the prospect of working as a technical consultant. I had never been on a movie set. And, of course, there was the whole ego boost.

"But why, Hannah? Why? Didn't Edgar Bronfman like Sterling's script? I thought it was going well."

"It's nothing to do with the script, "Hannah replied. "The Pentagon has blackmailed him."

"The Pentagon?" I was confused. "What do they have to do with the movie?"

"They claim the movie will be anti-war, anti-military. Did you know the military's PX and commissaries are the second largest retail outlets in the world, second only to Sears Roebuck?

They have threatened to have all Seagram's products banned if the movie goes ahead."

"Oh, no! Have you told Robin yet?"

"He knows. Of course we are all upset."

I hung up, shattered. Whenever I found myself riding high, I seemed to crash back to earth. Thinking the good times would never end, I had been spending money like crazy. The 'Thunderball' fiasco had cost a bundle and, that very morning, I had told Leon I would buy one of his Pocono Mountain Resort's limousines.

I suspected that he and Brooke had gone broke with the resort. He was now working in his family's import business in New York. The Hallandale house, although having the obligatory swimming pool, was quite modest. Like so many in Florida, it sat on a narrow canal.

It had been three weeks since I accepted his invitation to move in and during that time, he kept flying to and from New York for work. I was company for Brooke while Leon was away and she and I had finally become friends. There wasn't much to do and we did it together. Mostly, we sunbathed and played backgammon around the pool. I enjoyed her quick brain, her sharp sense of humor, and we laughed and drank the days away. Glen was almost four. A sweet child, he was not much trouble. An older woman came in daily and did the housework.

When Leon was home, he did a nightly Bar-B-Q and Brooke made a salad. If he was gone, we usually jumped into the El Dorado and Brooke drove us to the local restaurants.

Pleasant as it was, this prolonged period of idleness was beginning to pall. I decided it was time to move out and put some structure into my life. That was why I bought the limo. I didn't drive and, once I moved, I would not have Brooke to drive me places. Besides, I suspected Leon now regretted inviting me home. Maybe he had anticipated a threesome with two beautiful women. Late one night while on his way to the toilet, he detoured through the bedroom that I shared with Glen. I awoke to find a male appendage uncomfortably close to my mouth. My rebuff displeased him and he left, huffily adjusting his pants. I never reported the incident to Brooke but his attitude cooled after that.

Admittedly, Brooke and I did addictively play backgammon, often late into the night, and Leon frequently sulked off to bed alone. A rift was appearing in their marriage and my presence only acerbated it.

With the house-hunting going nowhere, I compromised by leasing a one bedroom apartment in North Miami for six months. Next, I advertised for a limousine driver.

Brooke never indulged in sport and I was craving some physical exercise. The advertisement read: 'Driver wanted. Must hold a limousine license and be available six days a week. Uniform provided. Don't apply if you can't play tennis.'

The day I moved out, Leon sighed with relief, insinuating that I had undermined Brooke's affection for him. He angrily blamed me for her constant drinking. As much as I had enjoyed Brooke's stimulating company, I was anxious to go. My pet hate was cigarette smoke and Brooke smoked like a steam train on an uphill climb. Furthermore, I was uncomfortable with her maternal shortcomings. On one occasion, when Glen would not eat his dinner, she had twisted his ear until the side of his face turned red. It was one of the few times we had words.

The rented apartment was in a complex called Coral Isles. It was comprised of four identical, hi-rise buildings on the bank of another of Miami's myriad canals. It too was a narrow canal but when the word 'waterfront' was attached to any real estate, the price skyrocketed.

I had the limo delivered to my parking spot. The first night in the apartment, I slept on the floor. Forgetting my plans to conserve money, I quickly spent a fortune making the place 'livable'. Tradesmen swarmed in and out like busy ants. Those white walls just *HAD* to be papered, or covered with mirror. Those plastic light shades *HAD* to go. A chandelier fit for a grand theater foyer was hung in the living room. An elegant, white Italian dining set with golden upholstery was delivered, along with a white plush sofa. Mirror-tiled containers were placed in corners, filled with artificial, white lilies. I was about to rip out the abhorrent, yellow shag and replace it with white carpet when a prick of sanity prevailed. Three nights later, I regretted that restraint.

I had bought a pair of love birds to keep me company. After another busy day of rearranging furniture and interviewing prospective chauffeurs, I let my housemates out of their cage. Relaxing in the soothing ambience of my creation, I opened a bottle of Bordeaux wine and dimmed the lights. The strains of Julie London's sexy voice lulled me as she sang 'Cry Me a River'.

Eventually, hunger stirred me and I threw a filet steak on the grill. It smelled delicious as Julie started her next track.

I must have dozed off. The screaming smoke alarm woke me. I leaped up, knocking over my glass of red wine. After running to switch off the stove I grabbed the broom and banged violently on the plastic alarm box. My beautiful apartment was filled with smoke. Coughing, I ran to the balcony and shoved the glass doors open. Immediately, one bird waved goodbye, its eyes watering as he shot across the balcony and swooped low over the canal. I slammed the door shut just in time to stop his mate from following. This must have enraged Number Two because he refused to go back into his cage.

I cussed him and threw the blackened steak into the bin. Julie was now repeating the word 'cry' over and over. After turning on the noisy stove exhaust, I collapsed with the last of the wine and a handful of cheese.

Before going to bed, I made one more attempt to cage my remaining housemate. Grabbing a towel, I chased him as he defiantly thumbed his beak at me and darted from swinging chandelier to gilded mirror to curtain tops.

In the ensuing 'catch-me-if-you-can', I fell over the bird cage. Bird seed splattered throughout the room like buckshot from a hot barrel. Quickly it found its hiding places between elongated threads of the hated shag carpet.

The next morning, I was again on my hands and knees, picking up birdseed when the doorbell rang. Slightly bedraggled, I opened the door and saw this stunningly beautiful woman staring at me. I pushed a wayward strand of hair from across my nose.

"Yes?"

"Have I come to the wrong place? I was answering an advert for a job," she purred.

I looked at her exquisite features; her long, shiny black hair and my brain froze.

"What job?"

"For a chauffeur. I must have made a mistake."

"Oh no." I collected myself. "You've come to the right place. But surely you don't hold a limousine license?"

"I do."

"Well, I wasn't expecting a girl . . . . a, a woman."

She looked disappointed. "That's a pity. I'm a good tennis player," she added. I was still staring at her. She could have passed for Elizabeth Taylor's younger sister. I hesitated. I liked her instantly but did I need the competition of such a raving beauty? Alongside her, I felt positively plain.

"You would have to wear a uniform," I said.

"Of course."

"Then come downstairs and I'll show you the vehicle. If you have the time now, you can drive me to the tailor's shop and we'll order your uniform . . . what is your name again?"

"Jackie."

"I think we'll make a great pair, Jackie."

CHAPTER 16

I was trying to ignore the old men who kept deliberately splashing me as they swam past in the Coral Isles swimming pool. It was difficult to read when they continually tried to get my attention, hoping to engage me in mundane conversation. I lowered the back of the chaise lounge, rolled onto my tummy, and propped myself up on my elbows. I had quickly surmised that I was the only tenant younger than sixty in the old folk's complex.

The TV commercials which had lured me to Florida showed young people frolicking in surf and on sand with beautiful, sun-tanned bodies. Belatedly I learned that Florida was the retirement mecca of the United States. The commercials had omitted the hordes of elderly who made up the majority of Floridians. They emerged each evening at 5:00 p.m. to line up outside popular restaurants like a serpentine that went on for blocks. In winter, the peak season, their numbers exploded as so-called 'snowbirds' from the frozen north joined them.

My breasts overflowed the dazzlingly bright orange bikini. Maybe, with my back turned, the old men would leave me alone. I lay the book on the ground and picked up a tube of sun screen.

"I've just finished reading that," said a pleasant voice. "Are you enjoying it?"

The words surprised me. The book was hardly a bestseller, being a technical look at the measurement of brain waves, a subject that was still pretty new and one I found fascinating . . . if I concentrated.

I looked up into the engaging face of a short, bald-headed man. Maybe it was the surprise that he had read that rather obscure book; maybe it was his pleasing voice, his sparkling eyes. But, whatever it was, I liked him immediately.

He explained that his son worked in a Cambridge, Massachusetts clinic engaged in bio-feedback and had sent him that same book.

"Did you know you are the talk of the complex?" he finally asked.

"No. I know no one here."

"Well, you're quite a sensation. The mystery woman! You must realize, a young, glamorous woman in our midst with a limousine and a good-looking chauffeur arouses comment."

"When I signed the lease I didn't realize there were no young people here."

"Your frequent home deliveries from the liquor store and the florist add more fuel to the fire."

I giggled, amused by the trivial observation.

"What building are you in?"

"B."

"So am I and my wife. What number are you?"

"B314."

"Great Scott! Can you believe it? We're neighbors. We live in B316. I can't believe we've never seen you coming and going. You must come up now and let me introduce you to Harriet. My name is Sy."

"I'm June," I said as I adjusted my top, then followed him over to our building. It must have been about 11:30 for the same crowd I had seen the day before was milling around the ground-level wall of mailboxes.

"Mail time," he said. "The highlight of their day. Did you know that they place bets on which one will fall off their perch next?"

"That's macabre! I don't think I'll renew my lease."

As we climbed the stairs, we passed a plump, red-haired lady in a flowing hostess gown. She carried a casserole dish in her hands and was breathing heavily.

"Good morning, Mr. Saffer," she greeted my new companion. "I'm just taking some food to poor Mr. Stein in B230. His wife passed away yesterday, you know?"

Sy made the appropriate condolences. Once we were out of earshot, he whispered, "The casserole brigade will be marching up and down all day. Whenever there's a new widower, hordes of widows are instantly knocking on his door."

"You have to feel sorry for so many desperate and lonely people," I said. "Luckily you're younger than most of them." We had reached the top of the stairs and headed towards my apartment. Stopping two doors short, he fumbled in his pocket before knocking. The door opened as a female voice chimed, "Forgotten your keys again?" His wife caught sight of me and stopped. She had a dab of flour on her cheek and I could smell a cake baking in the oven. She hesitated briefly then smiled warmly.

"Who do we have here, Sy?"

"This is our neighbor, June," he replied.

"Then come in and let us get acquainted while I make some coffee."

I was bowled over. What other woman would find her husband bringing home a buxom, scantily-clad young woman and welcome her in for coffee?

I discovered that, like so many other Floridians, they were a retired Jewish couple from New York. Harriet insisted I stay for lunch and I ran next door to cover up.

Despite the age gap and our vast lifestyle differences, our values and zest for life were compatible. They became two of my best, lifelong friends.

CHAPTER 17

Jackie and Brooke

Jackie rarely started work before twelve. I liked to take it easy most mornings but afternoons were spent playing tennis, lounging on the beach, or playing backgammon at one of the many clubs I had joined.

Miami's night life was raging and I was really getting into the club scene; looking for a prospective husband of course, although the more fun I had, the less I thought of those poor, homeless orphans. During the seventies, the most popular club acts were Sonny and Cher or Tina Turner.

Jackie and I became accustomed to the stir we created wherever we went. Limousines were not uncommon in Miami or Main Beach but, immodestly, I believe it was the driver and passenger who caused the stir. Adding to our profile was a furled flag on the front of the limo. Prior to being bought by Leon, and then me, the limousine had belonged to a foreign diplomat. Rather than remove the flag, Leon had kept it furled inside a cover. I threw away the cover and replaced the flag with one reading 'The Khaki Mafia,' which fluttered in the wind. The gawking onlookers probably thought we were a pair of gangster's molls, after reading those three words, unless they had been discerning enough to have read the book, of course.

I designed Jackie's uniform; a black one-piece, snug-fitting, hot-pants suit zippered up the front. The words The Khaki Mafia were emblazoned in red letters above the right breast. Her image was further enhanced with a small black cap and shiny, knee-high, patent-leather boots.

Aware that too many of my dates were showing too much interest in my driver, I did my best to compete. Between my suntanned, blonde good looks and her pale skin and raven hair, people gaped and cars occasionally ran into each other as she helped me to alight.

Besides driving and playing tennis, Jackie's main job was to keep the champagne bucket filled with ice. By lunch time, I had often sampled the champagne. I wasn't necessarily in need of a drink but, if I allowed the ice to melt, I would be disrespecting her job performance.

Jackie never drank so that left me without a drinking mate. Consequently, I frequently had her drive me over to Brooke's place in Hallandale. By that time, Brooke's marriage was even rockier than when I left. Leon had banned me from his house, blaming me for Brooke's downfall. No problem! I had Jackie pull into their driveway and summons Brooke to the car. We wiled away many a pleasant afternoon playing backgammon in the back seat while demolishing a bottle of gin. The hot rock music, blasting from our limo, drew bemused neighbors to their windows.

My resolve to change my ways was obviously tottering and dreams of that child were dissolving. Once again, I had fallen into that party girl mode. Maybe I just wasn't 'marriage material'.

There was no shortage of dates but if I mentioned marriage and adoption, my dates all dropped me quicker than a handful of cow dung. Adoption looked as remote as any chance I had of becoming an astronaut.

One day, Jackie drove me to a suburban post office so I could mail a birthday card to my mother. It was about one o'clock when she pulled up in front of the small, red brick building. A curious crowd gathered around, staring as she stepped out in her shiny black, figure-hugging suit. With her long hair flying in the wind, she looked as if she had just stepped off the cover of one of those romance novels. She opened the rear door and I—holding the card in one hand and a glass of champagne in the other—tumbled out in my equally figure-hugging, split-to-the-crotch, white dress. Jackie steadied me and the spectators parted as, head held high, I staggered through their midst, oblivious to their raised eyebrows. Those were the days before movie stars like Lindsay Lohan behaved badly so maybe I set the precedence.

As we drove away, I said, "We need to stop by the apartment while I pick up another bottle of champagne. I'm bored."

"Do you want a game of tennis?" Jackie asked.

"No. After I pick up the champagne, drive me to Dania. I want to go to that UHF television studio."

"You mean Channel 51? Whatever for? Their shows are all in Spanish." Her observation was indeed correct. The station in question catered to the large Hispanic population in Dade and Broward counties.

"Yes. It's time they added a talk show," I replied. "Most of the Hispanics speak English so I'm going to start my own talk show."

"When did this happen?"

"Five minutes ago."

"Have you ever hosted a TV show? Who will sponsor you?"

"Don't bother me with trivia. I'm a saleswoman. I'll sell advertising to pay for my air time. I need a challenge."

Jackie shook her head. "Are you cancelling today's flying lesson then?"

"Oh. I forgot. Let's do both." I laughed, before prudently tipping the remainder of my champagne into the ice bucket.

A week later, we pulled into Brooke's driveway and Jackie tooted the horn. Brooke ambled out, covered in suntan oil and carrying the gin bottle.

"No drinking today, Brooke," I said. "I'm here on serious business."

"Pray tell," she said, climbing into the back seat.

"Seriously. I've bought air time on Channel 51 and I have a job for you. How would you like to drum up some sponsors for me? You've got the right credentials—good looks—and I'll pay you."

"You're joking. I've never sold anything in my life."

"And I've never hosted a TV talk show but we can do anything we set our minds to."

"I don't like getting up early." She tossed her honey-colored curls.

"You work your own hours. I'll pay you commission."

She seemed to think it over before replying.

"Well. I could give it a try. It'll get me out of the house. To tell you the truth, I overheard Leon telling his attorney that I drink too much and I neglect Glen. I might need money. I think he's preparing to divorce me."

"If it comes to that, I can tell you something that might help you."

"Tell me. Tell me."

"Let's see what happens first."

Within weeks, I started my first show and it was more enjoyable than anything I had done since quitting dancing. While I did not pose a threat to Johnny Carson, I was building a local following. Being UHF, we were only seen on both coasts of Florida, in Atlanta, Georgia and The Bahamas. Fortunately, I was doing okay with the sponsors who, as I recall, were a large furniture store, a hairdressing chain, a chiropractor and a day-care center. Brooke and I worked together the first few days, traveling about in her blue Cadillac with the overflowing ashtrays. However, it soon became too much for her and I was left to do the selling myself.

The shows could have been forerunners to today's reality shows. I interviewed self-made millionaires, models, crime victims, strippers, street bums and any interesting people living an alternate life style; it varied from week to week. I tried to keep it humorous and it sometimes degenerated into outrageous.

After several successful months, I decided I needed an address more in keeping with my lifestyle than the retirement haven for the elderly. Brooke agreed as we walked along the busy waterfront of Ft. Lauderdale discussing my future.

"I'm hungry," I said. "Let's go for lunch."

"Not today. I fancy fish and chips. Why don't we just buy some takeaway and sit out here and eat it."

"That's the Aussie in you coming out. But they don't wrap them in newspaper over here."

Fifteen minutes later, we sat on a bench eating our Skipper's lunch out of cardboard boxes.

"How are you and Leon getting on?" I asked in between bites.

Brooke threw a chip to a seagull before answering. A whole flock of birds swooped around us so I, too, engaged in her largesse.

"He's in New York. Spending more and more overnights there but we are still hanging in. I think it's a bit better since you and I stopped playing backgammon in the driveway. You still haven't told me your big secret about him."

"Not unless you're getting a divorce."

"Well I doubt you can shock me. We had a teen-age live-in house girl while I was pregnant with Glen. The day after I'd given birth, she came to the hospital and confessed my husband had been screwing her."

"So that's why you have such an ugly hou . . . . Oh! Oh, look at that!"

"Look at what?"

"That! Isn't it beautiful?"

She glanced in the direction I was pointing. "Look at what? Are you talking about that floating real estate office?"

"What else? It's magnificent!"

"Hell! It's an eyesore and they're a bunch of shysters selling worthless land out in the Everglades. Gullible tourists fall for anything."

"I'm not going to the Everglades, you idiot. I want to buy that office."

"That floating monstrosity?"

"She's beautiful. Come on." I jumped up and threw the last of my fish and chips to the birds. Brooke stuffed three chips into her mouth and followed me, grumbling through a mouthful of masticated potato.

I hurried towards the eye-popping, two-story Japanese temple. It was tied by heavy rope to several cleats. Stopping in front of it, I caught my breath. She was everything I longed for . . . almost as good as a Chinese junk. A rock pool ran the length of the front deck. The re-circulating stream was filled with water hyacinth and spanned by an arced, Japanese bridge. I could see a pagoda presiding over the top deck.

"Stop swooning," Brooke panted as she caught up with me. "Is this going to be another bloody 'Thunderball' fiasco? Anyway, it's probably not for sale."

"Everything's for sale if the price is right," I corrected her.

Reluctantly, she followed me across the small Japanese bridge and through the open door. Again I stopped, stunned into temporary silence. The interior was exotic and spacious. It measured about sixty feet long by twenty feet wide with no dividing partitions. Windows were paneled, the Japanese style that I was familiar with from my year spent there. Oriental plaques and ornaments hung from the red, grass-cloth-covered walls. Matching red carpet was underfoot and here and there sat small seating arrangements of black bamboo furniture. Dozens of pedestals stood like black sentries along the length of each wall. Plexiglas cubes topped these, protecting more small artifacts. The place looked like a cross between a museum and a whorehouse.

Brooke bumped into me and cussed. The lone man at the large desk in the corner looked up . . . and stared.

"What's he staring at?" Brooke hissed.

"Us, I suppose. I guess we do look a sight in our matching gold spandex tights and our skimpy fuchsia tops."

"How was I to know you were going to wear your spandex pants the same as mine?"

"How can I help you ladies?" The potbellied salesman with slicked-down hair smirked. Before I could answer, he added, "Are you here for a free ride in our helicopter? We fly all our customers out to our development by helicopter. It's quite a thrill." He stood, beckoning us over.

"I'm Tony." He stretched out his hand and I shook it. While I wiped his sweat onto my tights, he pointed at a large map sitting on an easel.

"This here shows the few plots still available." He started his spiel without looking at me. Brooke had wandered off to inspect the wall hangings and his eyes were glued to her behind.

"I'm not looking for land plots," I snapped, but he must not have heard me because he continued talking about roads and clubhouses.

"You can keep your plots," I cut in ungraciously. "And I've flown in a million helicopters. If you can stop ogling my friend's behind for a moment, I'd like to know how much you want for this place."

"What?" He finally dragged his glazed eyes back to look at me.

"I, I don't think it's for sale," he stammered. "I would have to ask my boss and he's out at the site today."

"Well you do that and I'll come back tomorrow for his answer. By the way, how many plots of land do you have left in Alligator Alley?"

His interest perked up. "Er, er, we are almost sold out. And please don't refer to it as Alligator Alley. It's a great deal. Are you sure you don't want to see one?"

"No, thanks. Once your development is sold out, I can't see that you'd have any use for this place. See you tomorrow."

CHAPTER 18

The phone in the apartment rang just as I was closing the door to leave for Ft. Lauderdale. I ran back inside. Robin was on the other end.

"I'm in a hurry, Robin. What is it?"

"You'd better make time for this."

"I'm listening."

"Someone else is interested in making our book into a movie."

"Oh yeah?" I tried not to get excited. "Who is it this time?"

"George Barrie, the owner of Faberge."

"Never heard of him."

"Faberge Cosmetics. Brut! The world's number one men's cologne!"

"Oh, sure!"

"Can you fly up here to meet him the day after tomorrow?"

"I'll do my best," I said, my interest surging.

I hung up and drove to the floating Japanese temple once more. The salesman had encouraging news. The owners would consider my offer if I could wait a month.

"A month is perfect," I replied, rising from my seat in front of Tony's desk. "That gives me time to find a new berth. I wouldn't stay in town here amid the gaping tourists. And now, Tony, may I have the grand tour?"

He grabbed some keys from a drawer and stepped towards me just as a middle-aged couple entered my soon-to-be home. Immediately, he changed direction to greet them with a smile as big as a split watermelon.

"Welcome folks. Have you ever flown in a helicopter before?" he began his pitch. "It's a real . . ."

"Excuse me," I interrupted. "I need the back door unlocked so I can go upstairs."

Tony glared at me, then threw the keys.

"Sorry folks," I heard him say as I unlocked the door and stepped outside. The back deck was just wide enough to walk around. The front deck, although much wider, was strictly ornamental with the artificial rock stream; nowhere to sunbathe downstairs. I climbed the steps to the upper deck. They were nice and solid. This time I would have the vessel professionally inspected before money exchanged hands.

The midday sun was blinding as it bounced off the white expanse of fiberglass which formed the upper deck. Squinting against the glare, I saw several green-tiled, hibachi tables scattered about. They were surrounded by numerous matching padded stools. The temple effect of the structure came from a small, centrally-located room with a curved Oriental roof. I tried the door but it was locked. Beneath the upturned eves were built-in speakers which led me to assume it was some sort of music room. Looking through the windows I could see it was empty. Instantly, my mind visualized it with one wall replaced by a chest-high bar and pull-down shutters.

I could envision myself and Brooke sunbathing topless, sipping ice cold gin while enjoying some funky music. A surrounding meter-high barricade, the ornamental roof to the lower deck, provided privacy . . . as long as we never stood.

The scorching sun sent me hurrying below again. Tony was now sitting at his desk across from the prospects. I walked out onto the front deck. The exterior walls were blue, an unlikely color for anything Japanese. I convinced myself the only possible color choice was fire-engine red. Despite the drawback of the hot Florida sun, the two 'roofs' certainly needed to be painted a contrasting black. And those blank, windowless end walls were simply screaming for attention. They could certainly be enhanced if I hired a painter to decorate them with a couple of fire-breathing dragons. The very thought of them dancing over the swells made me smile with pleasure.

Lost in dreams for my exotic new home, I almost forgot about my upcoming trip back to New York and the movie.

A few days later, I met up with Robin in front of the Faberge building in Manhattan.

"You're looking as lovely as ever," he flattered me as I climbed out of the taxi and pecked him on the cheek.

"I'm a bit nervous. What's this Mr. Barrie like?"

"I've only met him once. A self-made man. Not much education but sharp. He started from a shed in his backyard in the Bronx. His product packaging has been a sure-fire winner."

We had, by then, entered the building. A uniformed man held the elevator door back for us then pressed a button. The mirrored elevator was the most exotic I had ever ridden in and, as we sped smoothly upwards, perfume wafted in from the ceiling vent.

"Movie making is a new venture for him," Robin continued. "He has just financed 'A Touch of Class' with Glenda Jackson. Remember? She won the Academy Award for best actress . . . he made a killing with that one. Now he has read 'The Khaki Mafia' and loves it."

The elevator came to a halt as he spoke. The doors opened and we stepped into a world of soaring mirrors and gleaming chrome. Every available surface seemed to be mirror-plated, including the reception desk. I inhaled the same perfume that I had noticed in the elevator. A thin, blonde girl in a white mini-dress, silver buttons, and knee-high white boots sashayed out from behind the desk. She looked like a 'Bond Girl' and I was engulfed in a cloud of scent long before she reached me.

"Do you have an appointment?" she whispered huskily.

"Yes. With Mr. Barrie," Robin replied.

"Ah. You must be Mr. Moore and Miss Collins. Mr. Barrie is expecting you. However, his office is another two floors up."

"My mistake." Robin smiled, appraising her with lust-filled eyes. We returned to the exotic elevator, glided up another two floors, then stepped out into the exact same tableau; there was the exact same perfume in the air, the exact same desk, and the girl behind it looked exactly like the girl we had just left.

"Follow me," she smiled, leading the way without asking who we were.

After knocking on one side of an ornate double door, she pushed it open. I found myself in an enormous office that didn't look like an office at all. Towering glass walls exposed a breathtaking view of Manhattan. A man of average height, wearing denim jeans and a black T-shirt stood staring out the window with his hands clasped behind his back. He turned and came forward, hand extended. If this was Mr. Barrie, he was not what I had expected. His smile crinkled his well-worn face; I tagged him in his late forties. As he grasped my hand in both of his, he greeted me like an old friend.

"I've been looking forward to this meeting," he said, calming my nerves although I was still overwhelmed by the man and his surroundings. Robin and I had previously decided that he was to do all our talking. I knew nothing about the movie business and he did. Therefore, it was embarrassing the way Mr. Barrie kept directing most questions to me.

"Your story fascinates me." He stared at me from eyes like melted chocolate. "I'm anxious to get this up on the big screen."

"Robin handles the business end, Mr. Barrie." I lowered my own eyes, blocking his intrusion into my soul. This blatant absorption with me was completely unexpected. Had he become besotted just from reading about me?

"Well, right now, I want to hear more about your adventures." He dropped my hand and draped his arm lightly over my shoulders. "And please call me George."

"Well . . . George. Misadventures might be more apt."

"Do you have anyone in mind for the script?" Robin injected himself into the conversation.

"Let's not put the cart before the horse," George said, guiding me towards his desk. Poor Robin followed and sat down. I was unsure how to act and I continued standing, feeling awkward with George's arm hanging over me. Hearing an unidentifiable, soft whirring sound, I wondered what it was.

"Would you like the girls to bring some coffee, or maybe you would prefer a cold drink?"

The whirring sound faded, music filled the room and I gaped as the back wall slowly slid open, exposing an alcove lit by soft pink lights. A well-stocked cocktail bar came to a halt and it looked as if I was late for the party. Elegant men and women leaned on the bar or sat on chrome bar stools. Some smoked; others held a drink to their lips. It took a few seconds to realize they were incredibly life-like mannequins that would have done Madame Tussaud proud.

George laughed, pleased at my reaction much like a little boy showing off his favorite toy.

"Now what can I get you?" he asked, his eyes twinkling as my nerves settled down.

"Wow! This is stupendous." I gasped. "Better give me a screwdriver."

"It's a bit early for me." Robin was trying hard to be unimpressed. "I'd best stick to coffee."

"Come on, Robin. Live dangerously," I said.

"Yeah, listen to the lady," George agreed, winking at me. "She's not afraid to live dangerously."

"Oh well, you've twisted my arm. I'll have a scotch."

I watched George bustle behind the bar and prepare the drinks. He certainly wasn't handsome and yet I felt disconcerting electricity between us. At the slightest provocation, I blushed stupidly and groped for words. Maybe I was reacting to his immense wealth and surprising surroundings. Or maybe I was reacting to his open admiration—the 'me' he had read about in 'The Khaki Mafia'. I could tell Robin was feeling ignored. Such instant admiration made me uncomfortable, as if my reality might not live up to expectations. My trip to Hawaii had deepened the self doubts. How does one live up to an image once it is created?

George handed me the screwdriver. My hand shook and some of the drink spilled over the side of the glass. George laughed, took it from me, and ran his finger up the glass . . . then licked the liquid off his finger.

I was shocked to be so turned on by this ordinary-looking man. Yet powerful men had always been my weakness and, of course, money meant power. The knowledge that he had pulled himself up by the boot straps only enhanced his attraction. He was so down to earth, even a little humble, that it was hard to believe that he was worth millions. Poor, unflappable Robin was becoming unglued.

After half an hour, George glanced at his Patek Philippe watch and frowned. "I'm afraid I don't have much more time and there is still a lot I want to know." I wasn't surprised he needed to know more. We hadn't discussed business at all. It seemed like he only wanted to get to know me. He turned to Robin.

"What are your plans for the upcoming long weekend? I'm flying down to Acapulco in my jet, taking some of my top executives and their wives with me. We're staying in a newly-opened resort . . . would you and June like to join us? We can continue this down there."

Robin brightened. "Well, I have nothing better to do. What about you, Junie Moon?"

"Count me in," I answered huskily, my heartbeat stepping up a notch.

CHAPTER 19

The Floating Temple

On the flight back to Miami, I couldn't stop thinking about George Barrie and the invitation to Acapulco. As for the movie, nothing was signed yet and, after being disappointed once, I wouldn't get my hopes up. But I was dying to tell all the news to Jackie and Brooke!

By now, Jackie had become not just my driver but a friend. No matter how many of my dates chased her behind my back, she was trustworthy. Those dates soon got short shift from both of us. Unfortunately for me, she had passed her realtor's exam and would soon leave to start her career . . . it was time I learned to drive and replace the limo with a regular car. The recent royalty checks were growing smaller. I couldn't afford to pay a chauffeur twenty-four hours a day and I often found myself late at night without transportation.

At the Miami airport, I stepped outside into the welcome sunshine. New York had been freezing and I missed that mink coat that Robin promised to replace and never did.

"How did the meeting go?" Jackie smiled as she opened the limo door.

111

"I'll fill you in on the way to the apartment. But I think I'm in love." I laughed. "Or in lust!"

"Whew! Tall, dark and handsome is he?"

"No! Short, sandy-haired and ordinary! But toooo sexy and maybe just a little kinky." I grinned. "And very, very rich."

One week later, the houseboat sale was finalized. I had hired two tugboats to move my new home from the commercial waterfront in Ft. Lauderdale to a unique new tennis resort a couple of miles north. Unlike other local resorts, it had no golf course. Instead, there was row after row of tennis courts and a series of identical, two-story floating hotels. It was an immediate hit with the well-heeled. Chris Evert, then the world's number one tennis player, trained there daily, watched by a handful of privileged onlookers.

Living amid restaurant and sports facilities would be convenient but also expensive. I had looked for cheaper marinas but my vessel was too big. Elsewhere, I would have had to cut out pilings and then pay for two berths. The tennis resort's berths, built to accommodate the floating hotels, were wide enough for my floating home.

The day of the big move, Jackie and I timed our arrival to coincide with that of my new home. We left the limousine in the large concrete parking lot and hurried along the dock past the floating hotels. I could see the tugboats—one aft, one fore—maneuvering my temple slowly into place. The captain in the lead tug blasted instructions over a megaphone to the three young resort employees who waited on the dock. Several hotel guests, attracted by the noise, were standing on their balconies, watching. There was a false start when the dockhands repeatedly failed to catch the heavy lines. At last they succeeded and the ropes were twisted around the large cleats to the sound of a few whistles from the onlookers. Wow! My home would never go unnoticed. I thrust my chest out like a proud, new mother.

"I can't move aboard yet," I said, turning to Jackie. "The water, sewage, electricity and phone all need to be connected. It will be ready when I get back from Acapulco."

"You're living it up," Jackie commented.

"Above my means, you mean. As much as I hate to lose you, Jackie, I will save a bundle by driving myself. I take my driving test tomorrow."

"When are you moving into this . . . this . . ." her voice petered out.

"As soon as I get back."

"I'm not sure about your planned red and black color scheme and dragons." Jackie shook her head. "I don't think any adoption agency would view this as a suitable home in which to raise a child."

"Children from Third World countries have no hope. They get no government support. Just to have a roof over their head would be heaven to them. Anyway, I doubt it will ever happen. I can't find a husband. If it doesn't happen soon, I might have to go and live in Asia again."

"Won't the same rules apply there?"

"No. The stumbling block here is the immigration. Without a home study, I can't apply for the child's permanent visa and without a husband I can't get a home study. If I lived in Asia, I could just take the children home with me, like I did in Vietnam with Dong. I might not be able to legally adopt them but, depending on what country I went to, that might still be possible, especially if money exchanged hands."

"That would be some sacrifice."

"Not really. I like living in Asia. The trouble is how would I earn an adequate living? I'm getting a bit old to return to dancing."

"Well, you still look great. Maybe you'll find a husband in Acapulco."

"Pfft! I'm only going for four days. I'll be back before my next TV show."

"Junie Moon, I'm going into real estate to make my fortune but it's going to be dull after driving for you."

CHAPTER 20

Acapulco

I had flown in every kind of aircraft. Back in Australia, my brother Russell was a pilot, flying passenger planes for Ansett Airways. Before that, he had flown helicopters and many light aircraft, often with me as the passenger. In Vietnam, I had flown in everything from General Westmoreland's Beechcraft to the big Hercules C130s and everything in between. But I had never flown in anything as plush as George Barrie's private Lehr jet.

One hour into the flight, I had need for a toilet. A pretty, uniformed hostess led the way. She opened the door and I thought I had entered a movie set. The marble wash basin was topped by a light bulb-encircled mirror. You could have started a perfumerie with the dozens of Faberge scent bottles and lotions that were laid out. The only problem was, I needed to attend to business and I couldn't see a toilet bowl anywhere. I sat on a white, fur-upholstered seat to ponder the mystery. Maybe the toilet was hidden behind another one of those trick walls?

I ran my hand through the fur, absently enjoying the hedonistic feel of such luxury. My fingers encountered the hard edge of a rim. Frowning, I stood and stared down. Surely not?

Grasping the top, I pulled upwards. Sure enough, in all its glory, there shone the commode. I wondered was I supposed to sit on it or wear it.

I lingered awhile, sampling the various lotions. The atmosphere back in the cabin had been tense almost from the start . . . ever since George had introduced me to his wife, Gloria. I should have known he would be married. Yet he continued pursuing me ardently with total lack of discretion. His executives and their wives seemed to enjoy the drama as they waited for fireworks. My feelings were ambivalent. I felt sorry for Gloria—a pretty, inoffensive woman—who handled the situation by drinking too much. However, my pity dissipated before the onslaught of pleasure incurred from George's attention. I make no excuses that I was even 'bad' enough to feel excited, just like the rest of the group, by the possibility of a 'showdown'.

Somehow, unlike Robin's behavior with Liz, it did not seem that George was playing any cruel games with his wife. He was just oblivious of her.

"Move aside, Robin," George said when I returned, reeking of perfume. "June and I have things to discuss."

Robin stood, expressionless, and moved away to sit beside Gloria. The pretty hostess refilled their glasses. Gloria took a sip then set her drink on a small table, rose and lurched towards us.

"Did George tell you how we met?" she asked.

"No."

"Georgie, dear." She faced her husband with a simpering smile. "Why don't you tell June how you fell for me when I waited on your table in that café?" She bent and kissed his forehead. "It was love at first sight."

George cringed. "No one wants to hear that story again. Go and keep Robin company."

Gloria smiled and meekly wandered off, more out of her depths than I was in a world of money and celebrity.

After she left, George filled me in on a little of their history. They had married before he made his fortune; she had a grown son from a previous marriage. George loved his stepson and adopted him. Now in his twenties, the son held a high position in the company which would one day be his.

I wondered why George and Gloria hadn't divorced. They seemed to have nothing in common so I surmised it was because of the son.

That plane trip set the scene for the following few days. George and I were under constant surveillance. It didn't stop him from stroking my hair, kissing my neck, stirring our audience's anticipation of a hoped-for showdown. Yet they took neither Gloria nor my sides. I think they just wanted the spectacle of a good cat fight. It never happened.

We were housed in a series of villas—each with a private pool—around the perimeter of a golf course. I, of course, had to share with Robin. Fortunately, there were two bedrooms. Robin was unusually subdued.

It's funny the small things one remembers while forgetting much bigger things (like the name of the resort). These five-star villas had no music. I love music and mentioned it to George. He called the manager. An hour later, a 'houseboy' arrived with an antiquated, record player and a handful of equally-antiquated, scratchy records that could have come from the Ark. George was disgusted.

The next three days were endlessly exciting. Not only did I anticipate the sale of our book for a movie (again) but George's constant attention had me almost drunk with pleasure. He paraded me everywhere, introducing me to everyone as the heroine he was going to immortalize.

It seemed the entire New York social set and half of Los Angeles was there for the holiday. That first night, we were invited to a party at the home of an American billionaire. Set high in the hills, it overlooked the beautiful Acapulco harbor. The party revolved around the largest private swimming pool I had ever seen. Beneath the colored lanterns, beautiful people played hard and drank heavily.

I was dressed in a cut-away, gold lame swim suit that had never seen water. Hanging low on my hips was a long, black skirt, split up both sides and tied around the hips with the same gold lame strands. Bands of matching gold lame formed the hem. Every time I moved, I jangled from dozens of gold bangles which reached to my elbow.

George proudly escorted me around the pool, holding me possessively as movie stars continually ran up to greet him, no doubt all looking for their next project.

A good-looking man approached and towered above us. He was wearing a brass Montagnard bangle.

"Where did you get that?" I asked, knowing it could only have come from the boonies of Vietnam.

"Why," he drawled, "it was given to me on a recent trip to Vietnam. I was doing my bit, entertaining our wonderful troops over there."

"How so?" I prompted.

"A USO show for one week. You have no idea the experiences I had. Why, there were mortars bursting all around and . . ."

"That's enough!" George stopped him. "You don't know who you are talking to." He turned to me and said, "June, meet Hugh O'Brien. And Hugh, this lovely lady knows more about Vietnam than you could ever know so button up and stop embarrassing yourself."

Hugh seemed like a nice fellow but he was just trying to impress. He finished his drink, spoke a little longer then escaped. George and I laughed.

The whole weekend was one long party. We were invited to a dinner at another mansion leased by the actress Polly Bergen. She was charming but seemed concerned over my make-up. No doubt this negative interest was due to the fact that she owned her own cosmetics company. She dragged me from the dinner table into the bathroom.

"Wash your face, June," she ordered. "I just have to redo your make-up." And so she did before parading me back out for the others to admire her handiwork.

The day we left Acapulco, I was with George when the receptionist presented him with the bill. It contained an exorbitant, additional charge for the old music player. George hit the roof. He would spend money like water but don't take him for a fool.

We boarded the plane and were about to take off when Joan Collins came rushing out with her current boyfriend in tow.

"Any chance of getting a ride back, George?" she asked.

"We've got room. Come aboard."

It didn't take me long to dislike her. She was glamorous in a heavily made-up way; all foundation, teeth, gums and bright red lipstick. The whole trip she ignored the lot of us, even George, while she made out with her new boyfriend, never coming up for air.

After Acapulco, there were other meetings with George but nothing again equaled that. Robin and George could not agree on anything. I felt Robin was too hard-nosed over the bargaining table but maybe George did not come up with reasonable numbers. The movie began slipping away and neither man would budge. The deal collapsed and so did George's interest in me.

Damn!

CHAPTER 21

Party Time

After my Acapulco stint as Queen for a Day, I left George and Robin in New York and took a commercial flight back to Miami. My disappointment over a second movie collapse was only slightly eased by the anticipation of moving into my floating home.

Brooke met me at the airport with a bottle of champs.

"A little housewarming libation," she said, holding out the bottle.

"Good thinking. You'll have to help me drink it." I climbed into the blue Cadillac, gagging a little on the smell of dead cigarette butts.

"How's it going with Leon?"

"He's finally done it. Moved out and filed for divorce."

"Where's Glen?"

"With the nanny. Leon's filed for custody. Claims I'm an unfit mother."

"What rubbish." I held a linen handkerchief to my nose, buttressing my sense of smell against the stale tobacco. "Anyway, don't worry. I'll tell the court that he tried to wake me with oral sex while I slept in the room with his child."

"He did that?" Brooke's voice rose.

"Sure did. And Glen could have woken up at any time."

"Bastard! I think he's going to infer we're lesbians. He blames you for the marriage break-up."

"I think lesbians might do a little more than play backgammon all night. Don't worry. We'll take care of him."

"My lawyer told me to start attending AA meetings as a defense."

"Good idea. And maybe we should take a backgammon board to court. We can play outside the court room while we wait. That'll be sure to rattle him." I laughed at my own suggestion but Brooke only twittered nervously.

Twenty minutes later, she parked the car and helped me with the luggage.

"I can't wait to see how the place looks now it's painted," I said, panting as I struggled along the dock.

"Damn! Get a load of that." Brooke jerked to a standstill in front of me.

I bumped into her and put my suitcase down.

"She's absolutely beautiful!" I gasped. "Better than I ever expected. For God's sake! Just look at those dragons. They sure look real, writhing above the water."

"You couldn't have made them any bigger?"

"Actually, I had hoped they would be bigger."

"I was joking, but look at those camera totin' tourists. I've gotta hunch you're going to be seeing a lot more of those."

"You're probably right. Let's get inside and crack that bottle."

After one week, my new home was looking pretty much the way I wanted it. I had retained the red grass-cloth wall coverings, the Japanese windows and many of the Japanese artifacts. Most of the black display pedestals were kept intact with their treasures. The open space had no partitions; however, I divided two sections with fabric tents. My bedroom was contained within a leopard-skin tent. The back wall behind my bed was mirrored, of course. A faux leopard skin and dozens of cushions topped my bed. Huge jars of pampas grass drooped over either side, at times tickling me awake as the houseboat rocked. I don't recall what prompted me to decorate the walls with fearsome spears, knives and grotesque, New Guinea masks.

A second tent of white silk and red tassels formed an enclosure for the dining room. The crystal chandelier from the Coral Isles apartment hung above the white table and chairs, which were also from the apartment. With the wash from every passing boat, the chandelier tinkled and swayed.

At the opposite end of the long, main gallery, a miniscule galley hid behind a black, Japanese-style bamboo bar. It was barely adequate for preparing food for the hundred anticipated guests but I intended putting those hibachi tables upstairs to good use.

Brooke and I were sitting on a zebra-skin sofa playing backgammon, cooled by the breeze which wafted in through the open window. A half empty bottle of wine sat on the black coffee table.

"What are we goi . . ." A piercing whistle and a booming loudspeaker drowned out Brooke's voice.

"Damn that bloody Jungle Queen," I yelled, jumping up. The wake from the paddle wheeler rocked the room crazily.

The backgammon board slid across the table and the chandelier swung noisily in protest.

"I feel seasick!" Brooke moaned.

"Yeah! One day those gawking tourists are going to capsize the damn Jungle Queen, the way they run to one side."

"Complain to the owners, why don't you?" Brooke said, sweat breaking out on her forehead.

"What's the use? This is the sightseeing route for homes of the rich and famous."

"Then how come you're in it?"

"Isn't it a joke? The next point of interest on the tour is Kroc's pink waterfront mansion."

"McDonald's hamburgers Kroc?" She stood. "I've gotta go pee, or throw up—I'm not sure which."

"Who else?" I too stood and looked out the window as Brooke hurried away. The Jungle Queen had come frighteningly close this time. No privacy! A sea of Oriental faces crowded the rails, their cameras clicking away as a voice boomed, "And here on our left is the home of June Collins, a famous author. Reminds you Japanese customers of home, doesn't it?"

Didn't the idiot on the microphone know that Japanese homes were ultra-conservative and rarely painted? Grabbing a camera from the coffee table I pretended to take pictures of *them*.

Brooke returned. I surprised us both by ripping down my top while laughing uproariously. Brooke gasped then ran to join me, exposing her own breasts. The ensuing camera clicks were almost audible across the water. I slammed the window shut and we collapsed convulsively onto the couches.

"That will give them some fine holiday snaps." Brooke chortled. "Leon is right. You're a bad influence."

"Aw, come on. Remember Robin's motto: 'Ya gotta live it up to write it down.'"

"Yeah! Well, the good news is I don't see you being allowed to adopt any kids if you keep this up."

Her words cut my laughter short. "It's not gonna happen. I'm no closer to getting married. No one wants me."

"That's because no one can keep up. Now stop the damned floor from heaving or I'll have to throw up again."

A month later, my new friend, Larry Vita, knocked on the houseboat door accompanied by a large, stout man who looked important the way well-dressed, big men sometimes do. Especially if they are wearing a six-carat diamond ring.

Despite the previous night's late party, I had been up for hours. Brooke was still passed out on the living room sofa. She had been too drunk to drive home and I couldn't leave my guests and drive her.

"Can we come in?" Larry asked. "I've been telling my good friend, Alfred Bloomingdale, that you make the best omelets in Florida. Do you think you could whip up a couple?"

Mr. Bloomingdale was eyeing Brooke's prostrate body with raised eyebrows. Her mouth was open and one eyelash had become dislodged and was stuck beside her nose.

"Don't mind my friend," I said. "We had a party last night. She's okay."

I poured coffee for the men and set about beating eggs, unperturbed by the uninvited guests. Since moving into my floating temple, it had become something of the norm for innumerable people to just 'drop by'. As for Larry, he was a neighbor and my new best friend. A short, lovable, good-hearted Italian-American, he owned a houseboat manufacturing yard not far down the river. Being unconcerned with the social standing of people (I know I've said that before), I was unaware that Alfred was the owner of Bloomingdale's department stores and the founder of Diner's Card International.

The two men ate their omelets and, before leaving, both agreed it was the best omelet they had ever eaten. I smiled at their gallantry. We were saying our goodbyes when Brooke sat up, red-eyed and disheveled, asking "Where am I? Would someone get me to my AA meeting?"

Inside my floating temple.

The pond and rockery had rotted the deck and had to be removed.

Doesn't everyone live in a floating tent?

CHAPTER 22

Living It Up

I was fast overtaking Elsa Maxwell as the Hostess with the Mostess. The marina resort had a large parking lot. During the last party, my guests had filled it to overflowing. Mercedes' and other luxury cars were too numerous to count, not to mention one helicopter. Among my guests that night was a leading national television newscaster. Improbable as it sounds, I forget which one. I hope it was Tom Brokaw. Where these people came from, I often didn't know but somehow the word always got around.

Living up to my title as Hostess with the Mostess, I kept food and wine flowing freely. The word traveled far and wide and I was finding little private time. People showed up uninvited at all hours of the night and day. My friends were an extremely mixed bag.

I have always been a generous person with little regard for money but this constant entertaining was putting me in the poor house. The book royalties began dwindling after the second year and the television show was not returning a fortune. In fact, the more I partied, the less time I spent selling air time. Something had to change.

Brooke's divorce went through and I was named as a partial reason for the marriage collapse. Brooke chickened out about playing backgammon outside the hearing room. She managed to hang onto custody of Glen as long as she continued with the AA meetings. However, she lost the house and her settlement was pretty small. Brooke moved into a smaller house in a poor neighborhood on an even smaller canal. In order to retain the nanny, she had to cut down on her expensive smoking habit putting her in a grumpy mood which was only relieved by a few glasses of vino.

Her one enjoyment was found aboard my houseboat where she was spending more and more time. During the day, we suntanned on the upper deck until we looked like refugees from Fiji. Brooke never missed any of my parties. It was not unusual to have to call for help at the end of the night to carry her down the dock by her arms and legs. It was up to me to see she got home okay. I recall her constant and inebriated mumbling, "Get me to my AA meeshing on time."

Meantime, my friendship with my neighbor Larry continued flourishing. He was like a brother to me and we spent many a quiet afternoon sipping coffee and chatting. He seemed to be simultaneously fascinated and concerned by my lifestyle. A happily married man, and with another business which kept him busy at night, he never attended my parties.

I doubt Larry was taller than 5'2". He had a cute pot belly and wore a ghastly obvious toupee. His face beamed with the joy of life and presidents and street bums alike called him their friend.

Besides owning the houseboat-building business, Larry also owned a faux ship named 'Miss Florida' which was prominently moored at the 78th Street causeway in Biscayne Bay. Miss Florida, a barge which never left her moorings, looked deceptively like an ocean-going, luxury liner and was hired out for gala occasions such as weddings and bar mitzvahs of which there were plenty in Florida.

The office walls of Miss Florida were a regular picture gallery, showing numerous photos of a grinning Larry posing with presidents and movie stars.

We were sitting on my favorite couch drinking coffee near the open, shogun window. I was nursing a hangover. The Jungle Queen had already passed on her afternoon run so the only sound came from some nearby seagulls and the gentle lapping of a swell against the pontoons. I inhaled the fresh salt air contentedly.

"Throwing another party tonight?" Larry inquired.

"No. I'm only expecting half a dozen friends for a quiet Bar-B-Q. It's a full moon and I never miss that."

"I'm getting worried about you, June. How much longer can you go on burning the candle at both ends?"

"Until I'm burned out, I guess."

"Now let's be serious. I know that deep down you want to settle down. You told me you have to get married if you are going to be able to adopt a child." He patted my knee.

"It's hopeless, Larry. I don't want to marry any of the men I know. Not that they've asked me. So I may as well forget about any adoption plans."

"That's a pity because the reason I am here is," he paused, his eyes dancing madly, "I have just the man for you."

"Yeah? Really?"

"Yeah, really! He's an old friend and one of the nicest people I know. Better still, he hasn't been divorced long and he is definitely the marrying kind."

"Who is this paragon?"

"His name is David Holmes and he is loaded . . . truly loaded."

"Oh. Well with a build up like that, I don't suppose it would harm me to meet him. Does he like kids?"

"That I don't know but I'll arrange something and let you know."

"Truly, Larry, if you weren't already married, I would look no further." I leaned over and kissed him lightly on the lips.

CHAPTER 23

Television Host

"You will have to cancel your show tonight." I listened to the Hispanic-accented words of the TV studio manager. "The bomb did a right awful job on the building. There's no way it is usable this week, or even maybe next."

"What the hell?" I replied. "Have they caught the bastards?"

"Not yet."

"Probably racial," I said. "A lot of Floridians are upset over the burgeoning Hispanic population. I have plenty of friends who've left the state already."

"Don't blame me. Jimmy Carter reneged on his promise to turn back the Cuban boat flotilla," the station manager replied. "That hasn't helped anyone. I may be Hispanic but I was born here and we've seen an influx of Cuban rubbish lately. No one is safe."

"Yeah. That's America for you. 'Bring us your poor, your downtrodden'. Empty your Cuban asylums, your Cuban prisons. Jimmy Carter is a lovely guy but he's too weak to be President. Too weak to turn the boat flotilla back like he promised. That was a stroke of genius of Fidel, to empty his asylums and prisons and put the inmates on boats. He would not have done it if we'd had a stronger commander-in-chief."

"No doubt. Crime has increased by 500% in Dade and Broward counties. We're all suffering, though I doubt it was one of the boat scum who threw the bomb."

"Well, my friends are American. When they can't get a job in their birthplace unless they speak Spanish, you can understand their anger."

"I know. Anyway, I'm busy. Gotta get this mess cleaned up. Just needed to let you know."

Later in the day, I dropped by my old neighbors at Coral Isles for a coffee. Sy and Harriet occasionally attended my parties and I know it added a touch of excitement to their lives.

Sy was away, hanging a mirror in one of the other condos when I arrived.

"My show is cancelled," I told Harriet.

"Here. Eat some potato blintzes," she said, piling them onto my plate.

"The studio was blown up, apparently by some Hispanic-hating maniac."

"We Jews know all about racially motivated maniacs," Harriet replied, sitting down across the table from me.

"I might have to refund some of my sponsor's money."

"Pity! If the cameras and lights are still intact, why not do the show sitting on a blanket in the night air outside the bombed out building?"

I jerked my head up, swallowing the mouthful of blintz "A great idea but I've already cancelled tonight's guests."

"Well . . . it just so happens Sy and I have a police officer friend. He is full of fascinating stories and tells them well. Why don't we ask him to fill in for you?"

"Gee, that's a great idea. But could he carry the show for one whole hour? I tell you what. If you and Sy will come with him, I'll do it. You two are always interesting. How about it? I'll bring a hamper and make it a real picnic. We'll have wine and beer and chicken sandwiches. I bet the viewers will love the informality."

"Really? Wait until I tell Sy! We've never been on television."

"And I've had guests that aren't half as interesting." I wiped my mouth on a paper napkin. "See you tonight. Just hope there's no more bombs."

I believe that night's show was unique in television history, a definite forerunner to today's reality shows. As we sat on a blanket under the stars drinking wine from coffee mugs, the policeman kept us enthralled with his storytelling. Sy and Harriet added wit and laughter.

Later, viewers blocked the lines, calling to say how much they enjoyed it. No doubt Sy and Harriet were thrilled the next day when they received dumbfounded calls from friends who had seen the show. My ratings picked up for awhile and money was a little more plentiful. However, not plentiful enough. It was time to start thinking of a cheaper place to keep my boat.

CHAPTER 24

A Bad Move

Vic Starinki owned a Dodge car dealership in Akron, Ohio. During winter, he escaped the snow of Akron each month for a few days of sunshine aboard a small houseboat which he kept on the river in Ft. Lauderdale. I occasionally bumped into him as he visited the marina resort for lunch. A harmless, square, cheerfully-boring fellow, he was an alcoholic.

He was obviously intrigued by me and occasionally wandered onto my boat to drink gallons of coffee before heading back to his houseboat. During a sober moment, he once invited me to dinner. With time on my hands, I accepted his invitation. In a crowded restaurant, while waiting for the food to arrive, he threw up on the white linen tablecloth before collapsing in his chair. Rather horrified, I lifted the corners of the cloth and folded them over the mess. After discreetly explaining to the waiter—and tipping him well—I had him help me get Vic to the car. I drove my drunken friend home and never accepted another invitation.

Nevertheless, I am a forgiving person and poor old Vic was kind-hearted. Three days later, when he sobered up, he came to apologize.

"I'm returning to Akron tomorrow," he said. "I've sold the houseboat."

"Is that because you set fire to it while smoking in bed last month?"

"No. I just bought a waterfront house instead. I can't fit many friends on the boat; it's too small."

"Well, it's been an experience knowing you, Vic. Good luck."

"Another reason I came here is, uh, I was wondering would you like to move your boat and anchor it in front of my new house. I won't be there much and it would be good to have somebody to keep an eye on the place. You wouldn't have to pay dockage."

"Mmmm. That has possibilities." My brain was ticking over the number of dollars I would save. "I'll think about it. Give me the address. I'll take a look and let you know the next time you're down."

"Good. See you then."

I accepted Vic's offer reluctantly, not keen to move to the 'burbs' despite the money savings. Apparently the people living there were not keen to have me either but how they got wind that I was coming I don't know. I had invited Brooke to join me on the journey to my new moorings. She and I were sunbathing on the top deck, drinking chilled white wine. An ice bucket half-filled with melting ice sat between us; a couple of empty bottles floated, tilting sideways in the water.

"What is that racket?" Brooke grumbled as the tugboats rounded the last bend.

"It's only the tugboat engines. Relax."

"No! Listen! I can hear people yelling." She jumped up topless to look out. "Wow! We've got a welcoming committee. Get a load of this."

I stood to join her as she wrapped herself in a towel. A group of protestors milled aggressively on the waterway's bank, brandishing objectionable placards. Some were angrily hitting the air with their fists and they were all shouting at us.

"Go home."

"Not here in our back yard!"

"Take that monstrosity away."

"Don't devalue our homes."

"You're not welcome, you whores," one yelled, pointing at Brooke's breasts as her towel slipped when she thumbed her nose.

I turned to Brooke. "Surely that idiot Vic didn't tell anyone we were coming."

"Probably did. He's never sober. Anyway, there's nothing they can do. Is there?"

Apparently there was. Within days, I was served with a notice to appear in court and fight a zoning infringement class action suit filed by the entire neighborhood

Several weeks later, I was sitting in the office of 'Miss Florida'.

"What should I do, Larry? They keep throwing eggs at my place." Emphasizing my words, I pulled a piece of previously unnoticed eggshell from my hair as Larry poured a coffee.

"You could fight it but they will be pooling their money and it will cost you a fortune to beat them."

"I moved there to save money, not pay lawyers," I groaned.

"The suburbs were never suitable for you," my good friend consoled.

"But it was free."

"You should know by now that nothing's free."

"You're wrong. Vic gives me a free demo car every three months. When they accumulate the miles, he sells them and gives me another."

"And you do what?" His brow furrowed.

"Oh, come on, Larry. You know me better than that."

"I just meant I thought you were leading the poor sod on."

"I'm not like that. I tell you what he gets out of it. Every time he comes down, he brings a bunch of his equally square, hard-drinking buddies. His chest almost explodes through his loud Hawaiian shirts when he brings them across to the houseboat to meet his 'property caretaker'."

"Yeah. I imagine it does." He straightened a black and white photo of himself with President Johnson then turned back to face me.

"Well, the best plan of action is to move before it goes to court. Why don't you move into the marina opposite here? They have berths vacant and you couldn't get a better, more central location than here at the 79th Street causeway."

"Expensive and not convenient to the Dania studio!"

"Bite the bullet! We'll still be neighbors. Only, instead of being my Fort Lauderdale neighbor, you will be my Miami neighbor."

"Ugh. I don't relish having to pay the towing company twice within weeks. I'm barely staying afloat until my next royalty check."

He sat down behind his desk and refreshed his coffee while I tore at a broken fingernail.

"Hell. What's wrong with me? I forgot all about introducing you to David Holmes."

"What?"

"The fellow I told you about. He would be perfect for you. He recently divorced his wife and he hates the single life. He could solve all your problems."

"Does he like kids?"

"You already asked me that and I don't know. He has none but he's a terrific father to his nephew whom he took in when his brother died."

"Well, he has to like kids."

"You need to give up on that harebrained idea. Think of yourself for a change. Anyway, in your present situation, it's never going to happen."

"What does this David look like?"

"Tall, fit and tan, neat gray beard, and he's a total gentleman. Loves sailing and spends six months of each year aboard his yacht exploring Mexico."

"Interesting . . . I love sailing."

"And did I say loaded? He's a multi, multi-millionaire."

"Then I'd best say goodbye to poor, wretched Vic and move down here. Do you know the marina owner? You might introduce me." I sighed heavily. "I suppose I'll have to pay to turn two berths into one. More bloody money."

CHAPTER 25

A Friendship Cools

David's home—unlike the luxurious white mansions that abounded on expansive lawns along the banks of Florida's waterways—was tucked away within a heavily-forested corner. As Larry led me through a back gate in the fence, I could hear squawking birds and screeching monkeys.

"What on earth is that?" I asked.

"Come look. He has a great aviary if you like birds. He's brought most of them back from his travels around Mexico."

"And the monkeys?"

"Spider monkeys. Not sure where he got them."

"I like him already," I said, admiring the profusion of palms and exotic plants.

The property was immensely private. We left the aviaries and headed towards the rambling, timber house. Just beyond it, I could see a magnificent yacht at anchor.

David appeared around a corner of the long verandah as we approached. He was smoking a pipe. I hated cigarettes but I could tolerate a pipe. He was barefoot, wearing chino's and a white T-shirt. My interest level rose.

"Larry, old man, good of you to drop by. Come on in."

Larry made the introductions; it was all very formal.

For a Floridian house, it was a bit dark inside with heavy furniture and timber walls but David made herb tea and was the perfect host. He obviously had many hobbies. One shelf was filled with camera gear and, in another alcove, I saw rock-tumbling equipment. An assortment of books was scattered on every available space. Although I found David extremely reserved, I liked him. He had an aura of dignified simplicity. We didn't stay long and I had little to say while sizing up the man.

"By the way, David," Larry said as we prepared to leave. "Are you free on the 28th of this month? I'm throwing myself a big birthday bash aboard Miss Florida. Half of Miami will be there, including John Knight from the Miami Herald. I believe you know each other."

"It depends if I'm here. I'll let you know when it gets a bit closer."

"Don't worry about bringing anyone. There will be plenty of singles. I'll sit you beside someone interesting."

David escorted us out through the back gate. As we passed the aviary, a parrot squawked. I turned in that direction, stubbed my toe on a garden edging, and cried "Shit!"

I did not miss David's disapproving stare.

After moving to the Biscayne Bay dock, I noticed that it had two advantages over my home's previous berths: no one took much notice of my rather unique home and I was no longer on the Jungle Queen tour. A semblance of privacy was restored and life began quieting down.

With a further distance to travel, Brooke stopped visiting as often as she had formerly. With Jackie gone and Brooke disappearing, I was feeling a bit lonely. I started frequenting the daytime backgammon clubs once more. Conserving funds, I had cut way back on my costly entertaining. I missed Ft. Lauderdale but, slowly, I settled in.

The day of Larry's birthday party approached. Although there were many gala events held on Miss Florida, Larry said that this was going to be the party to end all parties—in good taste, of course.

The day before the party, Larry dropped by to lend me some music tapes. "Can I invite my friend Brooke?" I asked.

"June, I don't think that's a good idea. The only reason I've invited David is to put you two together. This is one helluva opportunity for you."

"Aw, come on, Larry," I said as the boat rocked and the chandeliers tinkled. "She's my best friend and she's been so depressed since the divorce. The house she's had to move into is small and ugly and she can't afford a new car."

"Well, I'm against it. But, if that's what you want, I suppose it's alright." He sounded sceptical.

"Anyway, I think David might be a bit too square for me. Didn't you see how he looked at me when I swore?"

"How can you say that? He loves sailing; he loves the outdoors, birds. You've got so much in common."

"Yeah, yeah. You're right. You always try to help me. I wish you weren't married, Larry. You could help me adopt then divorce me later."

"Seriously, June, don't blow this chance."

"Whatever willbe will be," I stole a line from Doris Day.

The night of the big do arrived and Brooke pulled up on the marina dock in the blue Cadillac. It was belching smoke and not from cigarettes.

"You need to get that fixed," I called out as she jumped across the small space between the dock and my deck, looking very subdued in a navy-and-white tailored pants suit.

"Leon's gone all tight with the money," she complained.

"Well, come in. I'm almost ready. We can leave the car here and walk across. How come you look as if you've dressed to go to Sunday school?"

"If this David is as conservative as you say, I don't want to scare him off." She brushed past me, Chanel #5 engulfing me in her wake.

"Larry invited him for me, not you," I replied, fastening the last button on my gold lame jacket and wondering if, indeed, I had made a mistake by inviting her.

My misgivings increased as we passed by the battalion of luxury cars lined up in front of Miss Florida. Brooke's eyes gleamed as she smoothed down her short hairdo.

"Just as well I parked over at your place," she said. "What does David drive?"

"There was a new Silver Cloud Rolls Royce parked at his house."

Inside, we accepted pink champagne from the bartender and milled among the well-dressed guests, none of whom we knew except—in my case—Larry. He gave me a warm hug and I introduced him to Brooke.

"Let me show you your place settings," he said, taking my hand and leading us to the table. "Sorry, I have to leave you to greet my other guests."

"We're okay, Larry. Don't worry about us."

The long table was awash with silverware and vases of sweet-smelling hyacinth. Gold-rimmed place cards spelled out our names; mine was between David and Brooke.

"No one's sitting yet," Brooke observed. "Can you show me where the 'ladies' is?"

"Yeah. Come on." I zigzagged through the guests with her in tow. Inside the ladies room, only one stall was vacant.

"You go ahead," I told Brooke as I admired myself in the mirror. I was wearing black, silk pants with a gold, form-fitting Chinese jacket and long gold earrings.

Another stall became empty and I decided to eliminate any need to get up and go during the dinner.

"Are you in there, June?" Brooke called out.

"Yes. I won't be a moment."

"Look, I'm going on ahead. I hear they're sitting down already."

"What's the big hurry? I'm coming now."

Unfortunately, the zipper on my pants jammed and, by the time I came out, Brooke had gone. Feeling peeved, I washed my hands and hurried back to the table. When I got there, Brooke was sitting in my place, deep in conversation with David.

"I see you two have met." I forced a smile. They barely acknowledged my arrival as Brooke poured it on thick. David's eyes gleamed as he stared at her, engrossed.

"I think you're in my seat, Brooke," I said.

"I'll move as soon as I finish my story," she brushed me off. Fuming, I had no recourse but to sit in her vacant seat or stand awkwardly. David could not be called handsome but he was definitely quite pleasant-looking. Anyone would consider him a catch even if he didn't have all that money. But he wasn't the first wealthy man I had known and money had never been my priority. Stupid me . . .

The dinner seemed endless. I was barely acknowledged as they chatted on and on.

"Oh, yes! I love sailing!" I heard Brooke say, causing me to choke. Leon had owned a small motor boat and Brooke refused to go out in it after the first couple of times when she became violently seasick.

"Why don't you tell David about Leon's boat? About the time the head malfunctioned?" I prompted, leaning forward to see around her. "She had just vomited and, when she flushed, instead of the toilet sucking it down, it threw it all back up in her face." I chuckled nastily at the recollection.

David frowned.

"The ocean was particularly rough that day," Brooke snapped, turning her back on me. "And an aviary? How wonderful! I'd love to see it, David. I just adore parrots."

What a lie, I thought, watching David's total and utter absorption. She had been determined to catch him it seemed, even before meeting the man. Maybe the ailing Cadillac wouldn't be a problem much longer. I gave up trying to join the conversation and gulped my champagne down. Good men were definitely hard to find. Why had I hesitated over him being conservative? Why the hell hadn't I listened to Larry?

CHAPTER 26

Alaska Calls

I consider myself a passionate person, throwing myself into life with fervor. The same applies to conversation—I listen avidly to a good story and I am an enthusiastic raconteur. My mother constantly stated that a visit from me felt as if a cyclone had blown through. A conservative lady, I believe she meant it in a nice way.

So maybe I was too flamboyant to suit David. Despite my flamboyance, I was sensitive to people and circumstances around me, but I refused to become intimidated by social/political correctness. If I drank too much, I could become loud. Discipline and self control were admirable traits for military personnel but not for me. I believed that too much of either would stifle life's joie de vivre.

Robin's favorite phrase was "You've got to live it up to write it down" and I endorsed that thought, even if it was an excuse for life's excesses.

Obviously, I had lost my chance with David. I sensed that the very first day when I said 'shit'.

"I told you not to invite her." Larry shook his head while following me aimlessly on the upper deck. A rare frown crossed his face as I wiped the tables with a damp towel. He dodged a swooping pelican that splattered blotches of white crap onto a hibachi table that I had just finished cleaning. I glared at the mess and said to Larry,

"Damn! Why hadn't I said 'crap' in front of David? That might have gone down better." Larry didn't answer but my mind became sidetracked with the variations of shit words at my disposal. If only I had screamed 'excrement' or 'poop' or 'number two' . . . there were so many options that would have made a better impression.

It was midday and the sun blinded me as it bounced off the white fiberglass. I stopped and wiped my sweating face on my sleeve.

"I just never expected Brooke to come onto David like that." I picked up the earlier conversation. "She must be desperate since she got the short end of the stick in the divorce."

"Well it's unlikely you will get another chance like that one."

"I know. I know. And, yes, he's a great catch. But there wasn't any chemistry between us. Maybe I'm stupid but that is important to me."

"Well, Junie Moon, no use crying over spilt milk. But you still have a money problem."

"Maybe I need to take a job . . . perish the thought! I haven't worked for a boss since I was a teenager."

A speedboat shot close by and the deck rocked beneath our feet.

"Come on. I'm finished up here. I'll make us a sandwich for lunch."

A few days later, depressed by my dwindling finances, I invited a few friends over for dinner. During the afternoon, I busied myself preparing several salads; a green salad, a potato salad, and a prawn, cucumber, avocado and dill salad. The guests would cook kebabs on the hibachis.

Evening arrived with a full moon. Candlelight flickered on the tiled tables and coals glowed in sunken hibachis, filling the immediate air with the smell of perfumed wax and burning embers. My guests resembled movie stars in the romantic setting. Leaning against the safety barrier formed by the downstairs 'roof', I surveyed the scene. Men and women chatted in small groups. A few slow danced to the strains of Nat King Cole and others were still eating. One fellow I couldn't quite place finished his meal. Rising from the table, he removed the paper plate from the cane holder. Walking to the edge of the deck, he threw the paper plate with its remaining food into the bay.

"For God's sake," I cried, straightening up. "Where is your eco responsibility? We don't throw garbage into the water."

"Aw, come off it, June. It all disintegrates. Lighten up."

"I have rules here," I snapped in a surprisingly bad mood.

"If it bothers you that much, I'll get it back." He grinned, ripping off his jacket. As I turned to go downstairs, I heard a loud splash.

"Man overboard!" someone yelled to a backdrop of laughter. Seconds later, several more splashes followed as others joined him! I wished I hadn't thrown this party. I just wasn't in the mood.

Early the next morning, I was cleaning the galley when Larry returned.

"Got any coffee? How was last night?"

"Larry, I'm becoming jaded. I couldn't wait for everyone to leave."

"Well, I've had another thought . . . How's that coffee coming?"

I carried the carafe to the low table near the Japanese window. "Grab a couple of mugs while I get the milk and sugar, will you?"

After we were seated on the sofa, I sipped the hot brew then said, "Brooke didn't go home last night, she went somewhere with David. That woman is something else. I don't know how we remained friends for so long."

"Come on. You told me you enjoyed her company."

"I did. She is funny and smart. Maybe too smart! Maybe conniving is a better word. You wouldn't believe the trap she's setting for David."

"Now, now. Don't be jealous. And you left out 'beautiful'. Anyway, it's not like you to be vindictive."

"I know she's beautiful, Larry, but I've always hated the games women play. You know, she has never got out of bed before ten o'clock. David goes jogging at the crack of dawn every day. She told him she does, too, then ran out and bought a jogging suit. She says she now joins him jogging every morning and hates it."

"Get over it, June." Larry made a space on the table and set a briefcase down.

"You're very business-like this morning! What's this?"

He opened the briefcase. "Now are you ready to stop crying over spilt milk and hear my idea?"

"Shoot."

"I have perfected a new invention."

"Not the multi-level parking lot?"

"That one's already sold. This one is for low-cost, highly-insulated, and easy-to-erect housing."

"There's no doubt about you. You've always got so many irons in the fire."

He grinned while pulling out a stack of photos and handing them over.

I shuffled through the ten-by-eight, black and white glossies. One of them showed eight young men holding up a thick white sheet of material. It looked like styrofoam but a Renault car sat upon it.

"I told you inventing is my first love . . . how's that for strength?" Larry sounded pleased. "The material is light, yet incredibly strong. It has a superb insulating factor making it suitable for countries with extreme climates."

"Impressive!" I murmured, wondering what it had to do with me.

"Our motto is 'You can heat it with a candle and cool it with an ice cube.'"

"Very clever."

"I'm selling franchises to several countries where they have a need for affordable, quick housing. The beauty is that ten unskilled men with one experienced overseer can erect a house in less than a week. They are simple but perfect for the poorer countries."

"That's pretty neat, Larry, and I can see where they could fill a great need but why are you telling me?"

"This could be an opportunity for you. I have already sold a franchise to the government in Puerto Rico. I'm now trying for some African countries. It's perfect for any place with extreme climate. A place such as Alaska, and that's where you come in."

"Alaska? Me?"

"You are a good salesperson and you could make some decent money with this. I'll pay commission on the number of houses you sell. The Alaskan villages are so remote they don't even have roads out to them. We can drop these materials in by Chinook helicopters and replace the humpy's the poor damned Eskimos are living in now."

"I thought they lived in igloos?"

"Not really, but what's the difference? They have the money. Uncle Sam has recently given them hundreds of millions of dollars as compensation for the land we took from them in the early part of the century."

"I'm flattered that you think I can do it, Larry. Let me think about it. I haven't got a clue about Alaska and I wouldn't want to let you down."

"I want to help you, June. I know you're not making a fortune on Channel 51."

I nodded. "But I love doing it. If I go to Alaska, I'll have to pre-tape a show first . . ." We sat in silence for awhile then Larry rose to leave.

"I'll do it," I said. "I've been depressed lately. Don't know why but I've started dreaming about Vietnam again. Maybe I need a change."

CHAPTER 27

A Boy Called Benny

I tightened my seat belt as the Northwest Airlines jet rode the air turbulence into Anchorage. Would it be anything like Iceland, I wondered? Some years ago, I had spent a few days in Reykjavik during my travels. It was fascinating, looking like a moonscape in parts, but freezing! However, it was now June and I was told the snow would be melted from the ground in Alaska.

Weeks earlier, I had celebrated another birthday. It was hard to believe that six years had passed since I left Vietnam. I felt dejected when I recalled I was no nearer to my objective of adopting a child. Mentally, I chided myself for not trying harder to overcome the obstacles. Poor children were out there, starving everywhere while I was self-indulgently partying on. Adoptions were difficult for anyone and I was far from what would be considered 'the perfect candidate'. I felt sure many prospective parents must give up, frustrated by the agencies' stringent requirements. Everyone knew the stories of pedophiles and other undesirables who tried to abuse the system but I had seen firsthand the many children starving on the streets.

I had read books about Josephine Baker and how she had adopted twelve children. Her background had been similar to my own, although with far greater acclaim. She, along with Margaret Meade, was one of my two favourite heroines.

Mentally, I argued back and forth. If I jumped into marriage and was unhappy, the child would also be unhappy. One of my problems seemed to be that I attracted the wrong men. What I needed was a nice, stable, 'normal' man. Someone like David! The trouble was, such men bored me. Jacques Costeau would have been my perfect match but he was married and in desperate need of a nose job.

I peered out the window as the plane dropped altitude. We descended low enough to see the buildings of a sprawling town; the flat, brown plains and the gray waters of the Cook Inlet. More distant and much higher, jagged mountaintops glinted spectacularly in heavy snow. I easily imagined bald eagles encircling those peaks.

Before leaving Miami, I had visited the library and done research on the twelve Alaskan Native regional groups. The nine hundred sixty-two and a half million dollars the American government had given native Alaskans in 1971 under the Native Land Settlement Act was apparently disappearing fast.

Native villagers who had never had more than subsistence-level survival from fishing and hunting voted in the members—usually the village elders—to form the committees that would handle this enormous windfall. These simple, unsophisticated people had rudimentary education at best and certainly no knowledge of investments. The task of handling such huge sums was overwhelming for a simple reindeer herder or a spear fisherman.

Each group's share of the pie was determined by the size of the population within that region. Profits from the investments were meant to be split among shareholders—the residents.

Predators from the 'lower forty-eight' arrived in droves, behaving like sharks in a feeding frenzy. Lawyers, accountants, bankers, businessmen of every ilk came salivating at the mouth while smooth-talking their business plans to this easy prey.

With this new found knowledge, I did not wish to be perceived as another fast-talking scammer from down south. Sadly, by my arrival, only two groups out of twelve still had any remaining funds. Of these, I had selected to meet with the strongest, a group known as The Bering Strait Natives.

Stepping briskly through the busy Anchorage terminal, I stopped to stare at a towering polar bear. Its long claws and beady black eyes made me shiver. The taxidermist had excelled. Even inside the glass enclosure, it was still frightening.

I had always visualized Alaska covered in ice and snow so it was a surprise to step outside into a balmy day beneath blue skies. There were two hours to fill until my meeting at The Bering Strait Natives' downtown office. The open cab windows allowed me to fill my lungs with clean air. Curiously, I gazed at a sea of glass skyscrapers. There were green glass buildings, gray glass buildings, golden glass buildings—every colored tint of the rainbow—all blindingly reflective of the midday sun.

"Is this your first visit, Miss?" The thin, straggly-bearded cabbie broke my absorption.

"Yes. It's not what I expected. It looks a lot like Houston, Texas."

"Too damn right. It's those damned oil companies. Seems like they sprung up overnight." He slowed down for a traffic light and spat through his open window.

"Is it all like this? I was hoping to see something a little more rustic."

He grated the gears as he took off again. "Naw. These monstrosities are only on the outskirts of town. It's nicer in the town proper. And if it's rustic you want, you need to travel away from Anchorage."

The wind was blowing my hair about. I closed the window.

"Sorry, the cab's got no air conditioning," the driver chatted on. "That's the latest thing here. Those slick salesmen have flooded in, making their fortunes."

"That's a surprise. Back home we always joked about trying to sell refrigerators to an Eskimo."

"Yeah! But those glass mausoleums have all had to be air-conditioned," he said scathingly while squealing around a corner. "Anyway, where's home lady?"

"Australia. Do you know where that is?" I asked, expecting a 'no'."

"Sure. You got those kangaroos, right? And our countries share history. That water you must have seen while flying in is Cook Inlet, named after Captain Cook, the same one as found Australia. So is the Captain Cook Hotel where I'm taking you. We'll be there in five more minutes."

"I lucked out by getting into your cab," I flattered the little man. "You've enlightened me along the way and got me here safely. And you're the first Eskimo I've met. Are they all as friendly as you?"

"No. And I'm not Eskimo. I'm Aleut."

He pulled the cab to a halt and I made up for my blunder by tipping him handsomely.

With time to spare, I checked into the hotel before going in search of the BSN building. After finding it, I mentally marked the office location, before wandering back to the hotel. There was time to kill before the meeting.

Right on the dot, I returned to the timber, two-storied building and pushed open the heavy door. A young Eskimo girl with streaming black hair and western dress manned the front office. Disappointed not to find her in native attire, I gave my name and reason for my visit. She coldly directed me to take a seat and wait. No matter where I traveled of late, it seemed the world was becoming homogenized with people of every race discarding colorful, traditional dress for western attire. And American fast food had begun springing up in the most remote places. Flat-chested Oriental girls were getting breast implants, making their eyes round and dying their hair. Afro-Americans were straightening theirs. The world was losing the thrill of different flavors and I felt sorry for the next generation.

Larry had been unable to give me a name for this appointment. He merely said it would be with one of the BSN officers. I had read that the natives, understandably, no longer trusted the 'white man'. Even though I had confidence in my product, I knew a sale would not be easy.

Ten minutes past my appointed time, a slender, brown-skinned teen-age boy shyly asked me to follow him. He pushed open the door to a sparsely-furnished, untidy office. From a chair behind a large, battered desk rose a middle-aged, Caucasian man. Not what I was expecting!

"Thank you for meeting with me." I tried to hide my surprise.

We shook hands and he said, "My name is Doug. I have read your literature but there are a few questions, Miss Collins, so please fill me in."

As I removed Larry's information from my small briefcase, I said, "You took me by surprise. I was expecting an Eskimo."

He accepted the pamphlets I offered, frowning. "Inuit Indian, you mean. This group of people is Inuit."

"Oh, sorry. I knew that. I just forgot." I was flustered by my bad start.

"That's okay." He looked at me impersonally and I noticed his eyes were an unusual shade of gray. "I'm the only white man with BSN but, then, I've lived in Alaska most of my life."

While he studied the stack of papers and photos, I quietly studied him. His tweed sports jacket was embellished with leather elbows. The top button of his shirt was open and a tie dangled, looking as welcome as a noose. A few gray, curly hairs peeped from the vee of his shirt. Without looking up, he asked, "Exactly what is the insulation rating on this and how much do the individual sheets weigh?"

For the next twenty minutes, he shot questions at me without ever looking into my face. I wasn't sure how to handle all this impersonal treatment. The salesman's code—always sell yourself first—had for years stood me in good stead. Not this time! I stressed the benefits of being able to heat the houses with a candle and of dropping the materials into isolated locations from the air. Occasionally, he nodded and eventually he pushed the papers aside and said, "Young lady, I would have expected to find a man doing this but you seem up to the job."

I hated being called 'young lady' and immediately tagged him as an old-fashioned chauvinist. Didn't he know the world was changing and women were rising above the traditional, secretarial positions?

"Now, Miss Collins, I have your information. It could be something The Group might be interested in. I'll present it at our board meeting this evening. Be here for our answer at eight-thirty tomorrow morning." He stood and shook my hand. I left, worried that I had failed.

It was 10:00 p.m. when I picked up the phone. "Sorry to call so late, Larry. The damn sun is still shining and I didn't realize what time it was."

Larry listened to my report then replied, "If you can't get a commitment, I have a suggestion. In two weeks time, we are erecting the first houses in Puerto Rico. The African clients are flying in to observe. They are not yet convinced that unskilled laborers can erect one so fast. You should suggest that a representative from the native group flies down also."

"I will, but Puerto Rico won't address their main concern about dropping material into the locations by chopper."

"No. But you get them there and I can reassure them."

"I'll do my best, Larry. Now I've got to try and get some shuteye. God knows how with the sky still light as day."

"Pull the drapes, you dummy."

I arrived back in Miami without a commitment but I did have a promise that they would look at the Puerto Rico project. Larry was satisfied, confident the demonstration would close the sale.

When I opened the door to the houseboat, my phone was ringing. It was Eileen, an American friend from California. We had met on a plane the previous year. She had been returning home after a stint in India with the Peace Corps. I hadn't been to India and I sat throughout that plane trip, enthralled by her stories. I told her of my desire to adopt an orphan from a Third World country.

"You must consider India if you're serious," she said. "The plight of the street children there would make you cry. Many are dying of starvation and most are living in hell."

By the time we parted company, we had become friends and she had re-ignited my waning adoption plans.

"How are things in California?" I asked into the receiver while trying to remove my shoes with my feet. "You're not running away with the Peace Corps again, are you?"

"No more. I'm married now to a wonderful man and I love my job as a Special Ed teacher. But, June, I may have good news for you. Did I tell you I have an aunt who is a nun at a convent in South India?"

"I remember!" I dropped one shoe onto the floor and pushed the remaining one off with my toes.

"I've been in contact with her and she has finally answered my letter. With her reply, she sent a Polaroid photo of a little boy named Benjamin."

My heart leaped. "Oh, I have to see it. Did she say she can help me?"

"She said there are many little orphans around the convent. More than the nuns can possibly help. She says she can put you in touch with a reliable Indian lawyer."

I fell into a spasm of shaking and laughing, finding it hard to speak.

"Oh, oh. I love her! I must write and thank her."

"Slow down, girl. There are still obstacles."

"Like what?" I gasped, my thoughts tumbling over each other in wild exhilaration.

"You do have to get an adoption agency here to do a home study and they will require you to be married."

"Why?" I asked, sobering up just a little.

"Without an approved home study, the immigration here won't give you a residency visa for the child. You could live with him there but you couldn't bring him here."

"Oh my God! Oh my God!" I was still incoherent with joy, blood surging through my veins like a river in flood. "Send me the photo and the address, quickly. I've got to see him. Little Benny! Don't worry, nothing will stop me now."

That night, I did not sleep. My mind was full of little Benny and plans for making it happen. The parties would stop. I was getting sick of them anyway. My houseboat might even have to go. And if I had to marry, so be it.

Two weeks later, I was sitting on another plane, this time bound for Puerto Rico. I was going through the motions of my life but it was hard to concentrate on anything except that five-year-old Indian boy. I reached into the purse on my lap and felt inside, making sure the precious envelope was there. The plane hit an air pocket and lurched. I glanced across at Larry and smiled. He wanted me along on this trip because the Alaskan had already met me though I doubted my presence would help. The chauvinist had shown no interest in me and I certainly wasn't interested in him.

CHAPTER 28

Puerto Rico

Mid-summer in Puerto Rico felt as hot as summer in Vietnam. A group of us had been standing in the blazing sun for hours and I was wretched. Watching cement pouring from the mixer into metal buckets was growing old; a stream of sun-browned, muscular workers ran back and forth, carrying the buckets to the building and handing them up to a sinewy man atop a ladder. The bandana tied around his head kept the sweat from his eyes as he poured cement down a hole between the thick wall panels.

"This is certainly a change of occupation for me," I said to Nunook, the stocky, long-haired Inuit man standing beside me. He mumbled an agreement while wiping his brow.

"I've seen enough for one day," Doug spoke to no one in particular. Nunook looked relieved. Off to one side, the three-man group from Africa seemed quite comfortable in the heat and dust.

"I'll join you later," Larry called out. "I've made dinner reservations at a steak house. Meet me in the hotel foyer at seven o'clock."

"Is this restaurant air-conditioned?" Doug asked.

Larry smirked, then added, "You may as well leave too, June."

After taking a shower, I changed clothes and headed for the hotel's cocktail lounge. I needed a cold beer to replace lost fluid. Entering the dim lounge, I headed for a corner seat.

"Miss Collins! June! Over here!" It was the Alaskan, Doug. "Let me buy you a drink."

He was seated with his Inuit traveling companion.

"Thanks, I'll have a beer."

"Well, Nunook and I are having a Bacardi rum and soda. That's the popular drink in this part of the world."

"I'll stick to beer, thanks. But tell me, how do you two feel about Larry's project so far?"

"I'm impressed but still not convinced about dropping stuff by helicopter."

I peered at him in the low light. He was wearing jeans and a ghastly Hawaiian shirt. Truly not your ordinary run-of-the-mill, suit-wearing businessman.

"Larry plans to show you a movie tomorrow of it being done successfully."

"He wouldn't show it if it was otherwise," Doug answered dryly, his sarcasm irritating me.

He beckoned the drink waitress over. "Young lady, we need a beer here please."

I hated that 'young lady' label that he repeatedly used. He seemed totally unaware of how it dated him and made him sound condescending.

Nunook dragged up another chair. I thanked him and sat between the two men. After a little small talk, Doug spoke at length about the trucking operation he owned jointly with the

BSN. Nunook, a shy man, added little. It was not exactly the kind of conversation to excite a woman.

The drinks must have loosened Doug's tongue because, with barely a breath, he next reminisced about his days as a merchant marine. He told of living in the Russian countryside during the German invasion in WWII. His ship and its entire convoy, while carrying arms to the allies in Europe, was sunk off Murmansk.

"Did you see the movie Hollywood made about the incident?" he asked.

"As a matter of fact, it rings a bell," I replied.

"After every ship in the convoy except ours was sunk, we tried to camouflage it with white paint. When the paint ran out, we finished the job above decks with flour and water."

"Whatever for?" I cried.

"It was winter and there was snow and ice all around. Didn't do any good though. The Gerrys came back and found us. The handful of us who survived spent days, hungry and freezing in a lifeboat, before being rescued by the Russians."

"Why didn't you return to America then?" I asked, my interest in war history piqued by his tale.

"Couldn't get out because of the heavy bombardment. The Russian peasants shared what little food they had with me. We scrounged whatever we could—flesh from horses killed in battle was a lifesaver. Don't listen to propaganda. Those people were kind to me."

His affection for the Russians was rare in an American at that time of the Cold War. I was surprised by his stories and found his background interesting. Encouraged by his friendliness, I divulged a little of my whistle-blowing exploits. Gradually his attitude changed and he began showing me more respect.

As irritating as I found him, he was certainly different from any man I had met since leaving Vietnam. By the time Larry joined us, I was surprised to be finding Doug most interesting.

In my hotel room later that night, the words of a colonel, my lover in Vietnam, sprang to mind.

"June," he had said, "you will have a difficult time settling back into civilian life. Very few men will measure up for you as you have known *real* men and seen them at their best. Men don't know what courage they have until they are tested. Many never are tested and many more don't meet the test. No ordinary man will ever satisfy you again."

Past months and years had proven him right. This Alaskan was sadly lacking in the charm department but my instincts told me that he just might pass the test.

Over the next two days, Doug seemed to seek me out. By the time we were ready to leave, he changed his flight. His new schedule took him into Miami on the same flight as my own. From there, he would change planes for Seattle, en route to Anchorage. Neither he nor Nunook had yet made any commitment about the housing project.

Doug

CHAPTER 29

Getting To Know Doug

Larry stayed behind in Puerto Rico to see the job through. At the airport, my eyes roamed over the other passengers. Failing to find Doug or Nunook, I felt a twinge of disappointment. I boarded the flight back to Miami alone.

After the hostess announced we could release our seat belts, I retrieved my purse from under the front seat and pulled out Eileen's letter. For the hundredth time, I stared at the Polaroid square. My heart quickened whenever I gazed at the image of the small boy smiling beneath a tree. His dark face was indistinguishable from the black background of heavy shade; the white of his teeth was the only thing clearly visible. The first time I saw it, my hands shook so hard that I dropped it. When I bent to retrieve it, my tears fell like shards of splintered glass, marking it even as I smiled.

Warm with pleasure, I tucked the photo away. It was by now firmly imprinted in my mind . . . this was my son! I had been hoping for a girl but that was then. I loosened my seat belt and daydreamed of the clothes I would dress Benny in—the games we would play—the books I would read to him—and the hugs we would exchange. All I needed now was a husband to make this a fait accompli! As always, I completely trusted in the fate that had unswervingly controlled my life. My only confusion was that I was never quite sure where fate ended and God began or vice versa, or even if they were one and the same. Whatever, some instinct told me that there was a higher being and I was not forgotten, otherwise, why was I still here after all I had escaped?

During my primary school days, we had endured scripture every Tuesday. The preacher man had half a finger missing and he always seemed to be pointing the stub at me as he raved on about the wages of sin. His proclamations of eternal fire and brimstone failed to scare me. I was more interested in his knobbly finger stub. As soon as he turned his attention to some other recalcitrant student, I continued eating my contraband sweets.

My childhood memories were interrupted by a now familiar voice. "There's an empty seat beside me. Come on back." My heart lurched a little as I looked up into Doug's gray eyes.

"I thought you missed the plane!"

"Almost, I had trouble changing the tickets, but all's well that ends well."

I grabbed my purse and followed him down the aisle.

My excitement level rose as I contemplated recent events. The trip to Alaska, meeting this man, Puerto Rico, the photo of Ben . . . was it all one big plan? And why was I so interested in Doug? I had shown little interest in David who was a much better catch. This unpolished Alaskan and I had nothing in common. Trucks? I would rather a yacht any day.

Doug ordered drinks as I settled in beside him.

"Where's Nunook?" I asked.

"He found three spare seats at the back and he's taking a nap. We've got a long ride ahead of us."

After discussing the recent trip, Doug launched into another of his stories.

"This Alyeska oil pipeline is going to be the longest in the world to date," he said. "It runs from Prudhoe Bay to Valdez."

"Never heard of either."

"Prudhoe Bay is in northern Alaska on the Arctic Ocean."

"It sounds as distant as the moon," I replied.

"And in winter it looks pretty much like a moonscape. But Alyeska's pipeline will really put Alaska on the map. ATT, Alaska Truck Transport, will be hauling drilling mud up to the new wells being drilled. It's a gigantic operation. The only road in and out was hastily built and it's a shocker. I'll be importing truck drivers from the 'lower forty-eight', men who can handle mountainous terrain. The work is hard but they'll make unbelievable money."

The arrival of our drinks interrupted his story.

"Do you drive a truck?" I asked when the hostess left.

"Sure, but not recently. I'll be running the business. We start operating out of Fairbanks next week."

"You're so involved in this. I don't see you having any time for Larry's housing."

"If BSN wants it, they will put someone with building expertise in charge."

We were so busy sharing stories that it seemed we had barely boarded before the captain announced we were starting our descent. Despite the growing connection between us, not once had Doug ever flirted with me or shown the kind of interest that

I was beginning to hope for. He treated me more like a business colleague. However, in his unguarded moments, I had caught his admiring glances.

I studied his profile. Funny, I hadn't initially noticed how handsome he was. Maybe I had been put off by his abrupt manner. How had I missed those beautiful high cheekbones? I *had* noticed his unusual eyes. Maybe I had dismissed him because he was considerably older than me and shorter than I preferred.

"What time is your next flight?" I asked, causing him to look at his watch. I, too, looked. While in Alaska, I had noticed that several of the men seemed to favor these ornate watchbands, thick and chunky with gold nuggets and small jade accents.

"Nunook and I have a five hour layover. We won't reach Anchorage until tomorrow." He paused. "How about joining us for dinner?"

I gulped air then plunged in. "I have a better idea. It's late now. Why don't you change your flight and spend the night at my place?"

His face remained passive but he tugged awkwardly at his tie. "Uh . . . I would need to see if Nunook wouldn't mind going on without me."

The sun was just setting as Doug followed me along the dock. Biscayne Bay shimmered brilliantly beneath its glowing coat of molten gold. I sniffed the salt air appreciatively, delighted to be home. We passed the last boat and my Japanese floating temple came into full view.

"Holy cow, what's that?" Doug's eyes widened.

"That's your accommodation for tonight."

He laughed. "Well, this is certainly a new experience. Seriously, is that where you live?"

"Yes. Don't you like it?"

"I'll reserve judgment," he stammered.

Interesting or not, he was such a square that I was a little apprehensive of how he would respond to my home. I crossed the curved Japanese bridge, admiring the purple hues of the water hyacinth clogging the water below.

Doug was close on my heels as I flung open the black, entrance door. I heard his bag drop to the floor and the words, "Holy shit!"

CHAPTER 30

An Overnight Stay

The green digital numbers on my clock read 3:30. Wearing my silk, leopard-print pajamas, I climbed out of bed and crept barefoot over the long expanse of crimson carpet, heading for the galley. At the far end, under the corner window, Doug was lying on the leopard-skin sofa, one arm dangling over the edge. I tiptoed in behind the bar and poured a glass of pineapple juice.

I recalled how, upstairs on the deck, he had tentatively kissed me for the first time. His old-fashioned hesitancy was endearing and I was surprised when such restrained passion was able to arouse me. So why had I then pushed him away? Was it because I didn't want to seem too eager? Or had I become a calculating woman? Me, who never played games and prided myself on honesty! Me, whose time was running out to find a suitable husband! Doug *would* make a good husband. He was stable, a quality I seemed to be in short supply of myself. And he was strong enough that I was sure I could not push him around.

We had eaten a pizza under the stars. He clearly loved the night sky and the smell of the salt water as much as I did. When I removed a small piece of mushroom from his chin, the brief contact with his skin felt strangely intimate. We had polished off a bottle of Chianti and then danced a little; a slow, old-fashioned kind of shuffling. Then, abruptly, I had led him downstairs, showed him where the bathroom was, made up a bed on the sofa and said goodnight.

I stood looking at him, now sleeping peacefully, not snoring. That was good. And he didn't smoke . . . that too was good. In Puerto Rico, I had noticed him using a knife and fork the British way. I liked that. Americans looked so clumsy when they switched their knife and fork from hand to hand. These were all trivial things but they could be so annoying in a relationship.

As I watched him turn on the narrow couch, the blanket fell to the floor, revealing his jockey shorts and muscular legs. He was still wearing socks.

"What were you thinking woman?" I chided myself. He would be leaving for Alaska this morning and there might not be another chance. I sat the empty glass down and tiptoed to the couch. He stirred when I kissed his closed eyelids.

"What, what?" he mumbled sleepily.

"Wake up, Doug," I said. "You look uncomfortable. There's room in my bed. Come on."

He followed me docilely to the leopard-skin tent, not his usual dominant self. My hands shook just a little.

When I awoke around 7:00 a.m., he was still sleeping with his arm around my waist. I hesitated, not wanting to move, feeling extraordinarily safe. This feeling of 'safeness' was new to me. Thinking about it, I wondered where I had lost it. After searching my memories, I realized the last time I had felt this way was years ago in my mother's bed. I had lay there, warm and content, between Mum and Dad.

My floating home rocked slightly. Prolonging the moment, I relived the last few hours. Submissiveness had felt unexpectedly rewarding. Our lovemaking had not been full of innovative surprises yet I was completely fulfilled.

I sighed deeply and reluctantly eased myself out of bed to answer a call of nature. While washing my face, I heard him stir.

"Good morning, Doug," I called self-consciously, a little unsure of myself after our first intimacy. Returning to the scene of our lovemaking, I threw him a towel.

"I'll make us coffee while you clean up." Practicalities eased the moment.

"I'd prefer tea if you have any." He sat up and reached for the towel.

"Tea? I thought you were an American?"

"Can't Americans drink tea? My mother was Irish."

"Tea it is then. How hungry are you?"

"I could eat a bear."

"Tough luck. I'm all out of bear. Cold pizza or baked beans on toast, take your pick. I've been away, don't forget."

I continued with the banter throughout the morning, unsure of myself now that our relationship had changed. I didn't want him to think I was reading too much into it.

While I cleaned the galley, he folded the blanket on the sofa then sat.

"What is this?" I heard him ask.

I glanced across and saw he had picked up a snapshot of Benny from the table.

"That's my son," I replied.

He frowned. "You have an African child?"

"Would that bother you?"

"No. I'm just curious."

"That's good. And, no, he's not African but Indian. I haven't adopted him yet but I will soon." I took a deep breath and asked, "Do you have any children?"

"Three from my first marriage and a son from my second," he replied and I forced a smile.

"Do any of them live with you?" I prompted.

"No. All grown."

"But I take it you're married?" I tried to keep the sudden panic from my voice.

"Yes and no. We're still together but not for much longer."

"I'm sorry I pried," I said, feeling a slight sense of relief.

"Don't apologize. But tell me about your plans to adopt. It's an admirable thing to do."

His words brought a genuine smile to my lips. Most people thought my plans were crazy. By the time I drove him to the Miami airport in the demo car, I was again anxious, not knowing if I was going to see him again yet unable to ask him about it.

"I'll call Larry in a couple of days and let him know the BSN decision," he said, making me panic. I wanted him to call me, not Larry. I gathered my courage. "And if their answer is no, is this the last time I'm going to see you?"

"Do you want to see me again?"

"What do you think?"

He didn't answer. I concentrated on weaving the car through the heavy traffic. In silence, I edged into the passenger set-down zone. Again I was nervous and unsure of myself. We kissed awkwardly and he climbed out and grabbed his bag from the back seat. I held my breath, my heart slamming into my chest. He shut the door and headed for the terminal. It couldn't end like this! I sat there, watching his receding back as my gut twisted. After what seemed like an eternity, he turned.

"I'll phone you tomorrow night," he called. I was sure he deliberately made me wait.

"Bastard!" I said, under my breath.

CHAPTER 31

A Recalcitrant Tooth

My relationship with Brooke was definitely cooling. The added distance between us after I moved to Miami had been the beginning. My disapproval of her flagrant deceptions to trap David increased the gap and it hurt that she no longer seemed to need me. Part of her entrapment plan had seen her quit the heavy drinking. By now, she had packed Glen off to live with Leon. He was in the way as she focused on David and David apparently was not overly fond of children. My instincts about David not being the one for me were right after all.

Cooling did not mean finished. I still found Brooke to be great fun as always and we still met for a laugh about once a week. But we no longer shared confidences. She had become secretive. Her guard was up, just as it first had been when I unexpectedly ran into her at the Pocono Mountain Resort. It was obvious she didn't want me around when David was there. Did she think I might tell him things she didn't want him to know? I never had with Leon.

Doug had been gone a week and I was feeling despondent.

"Can you meet me for lunch if I drive up to Fort Lauderdale?" I asked Brooke over the phone.

"Sure! Where do you want to go?"

"Nowhere too fancy. How about that conch chowder place? I love their chowder."

"Alright," she sighed heavily, "if slumming is what you want."

I drove the thirty miles in Vic's demo car. I hadn't seen Vic since moving down to Miami. He never traveled south of Ft. Lauderdale, undoubtedly too drunk to drive that far. But still he generously allowed me to drive to Akron and take a new car every three months.

I wanted Brooke's slant on the situation with Doug. She hadn't met him but she had an uncanny knack for summing up men and their intentions. I sometimes wondered about that. She seemed to have the power to enslave men, a thing I thought could only be achieved with sex. Yet she achieved more by withholding rather than giving. One time, after too many drinks, she confided in me that she seldom enjoyed sex. Who would have thought it? She was tall, willowy and super-sexy looking. I wondered was it a case of men craving what they couldn't have.

We were seated on wooden stools around a rickety table outside the little chowder joint. The white wine was so cold that our tall, stemmed goblets were sweating. The waiter carried out two huge bowls of chowder.

"Not too hot for you ladies out here?" he inquired, sweat making wet patches on his blue shirt.

"No. And it's too noisy inside," I replied.

"I'll check on you later then. You might want to try a piece of our Key Lime pie."

I noticed the lascivious glances he threw Brooke's way.

"Thank you. That sounds nice," Brooke said and instantly followed her words with a little yelp.

"What on earth is that all about?" I asked as she covered her mouth with one hand and started patting the table with the other.

"My tooth!" she cried. "My goddamn cap! It's fallen out again. Send the waiter away."

"We're alright, thanks," I told him and started to laugh so hard that soon Brooke joined me. The gap in the front of her mouth looked incongruous in her beautiful face.

"When are you going to get that damn thing fixed?" I asked through my tears.

"As soon as I've got some money," she giggled, still patting the table in search of the missing cap.

"If you don't do it soon, David is gonna see you at your worst."

She sobered up. "You're right. But I don't think I've got to wait much longer. He's pretty much roped and hog-tied."

"How's that?" I groped about on the table, joining the search for her recalcitrant cap.

"Well, before Leon took Glen I used him as my excuse to send David home without sex every night. I told him the noise might wake up Glen. Eventually he became too frustrated so I gave in. But as soon as he fell into a sound sleep, I shook him awake."

"What on earth for?"

"I told him he had to leave before Glen woke up."

"Didn't he get angry?"

"He did. That's why I had to send Glen away. But it has paid off, the poor love sick puppy . . . Now where is that damned tooth? Do you think it fell on the ground?"

"Probably in your chowder. Watch you don't swallow it." I lifted my spoon. "How's the Cadillac running?"

"Hopeless! And I can't afford to fix it. Did I tell you David lets me drive the Rolls now? You don't know what a big step forward that is. When we go places, he won't even let the valet park it. He'd rather do it himself and walk a mile back." "I think I had him pegged right. Mr. Pedantic. Mr. Neat Freak."

"You're only jealous he chose me and not you. But, frankly, I don't know how much longer I can suffer on that damned yacht. That is the first thing that will have to go."

"That's cruel, Brooke. He loves that thing. Now eat your soup and choke on it."

"He loves me more!" she replied smugly. "Now, what was it you wanted to talk about?"

"Nothing." I no longer wanted to discuss Doug with Brooke.

The tooth cap was found in the bowl of chowder and she neither swallowed it nor choked . . . the lucky bitch.

CHAPTER 32

Goodbye Sunshine— Hullo Snow

Much to my disappointment, The Bering Strait Natives group did not go ahead with Larry's housing project. But he wasn't too upset. The Africans had signed.

Doug was calling me almost every night and our relationship was slowly growing long distance but I had no idea where it was heading. He imparted little personal information but finally he told me he had filed for divorce.

Things were slowly progressing with Benny also. I had hired the recommended lawyer and sent a retainer along with certified copies of all my required legal papers. Now it was hurry up and wait. The trouble was, if I did not get married, I wouldn't be able to get an approved American home-study. That meant I wouldn't be able to bring him to the U.S. and I would have to live in India. It was not my first choice but I thought of all the countries I had already lived in and one more wouldn't make a lot of difference. It would, however, mean I would not need Doug. I was no longer sure how I felt about this.

One month after Doug left, he called me late at night.

"Where have you been?" he sounded accusatory. "I've been calling for hours."

"None of your damned business," I said, not liking his tone. "I'm a single woman, don't forget."

He backed off but it was the first time I suspected him of jealousy.

"Anyway, why are you calling so late?"

"I need you up here in Fairbanks."

"Fairbanks? What on earth for?"

"I want you to go to work for me. Larry told me you could use a bit of extra money and the pay is excellent."

"Larry had no right telling you that. Anyway, what is the job?"

"Dispatcher for the trucking company. I need someone here that I can trust."

"For God's sake! I know nothing about trucking."

"Trust is more important than knowledge. I can teach you all you need to know."

I wondered was the job just an excuse to get me by his side. His next sentence dispelled that.

"I will stay with you, teaching you the ropes the first week. After that, I'm off to Hawaii."

"What? You plan to throw me to the wolves while you are off holidaying in Hawaii?" I spluttered.

"Of course not! I will be working over there for a few months. I just bought a small ship. A one-hundred-and-eighty foot, World War II Y.O. water carrier. I have to modify her so she can carry drilling mud to the offshore wells."

"When did all this happen? You never mentioned it before?" I was feeling confused.

"The oil companies have only recently started drilling offshore."

"I can't believe you would expect me to give up my life here in the sunshine to come and live by myself in Alaska." I choked in astonishment. "And isn't it winter up there?"

"Not quite. Look, honey, I know it's a big ask but I had hoped you might want to see more of me. That we might have a future together. That's what I want, anyway."

"How the hell would I see you if I'm freezing my ass off in Alaska and you're off sunning yourself in . . . ." Suddenly his words penetrated. "Would you mind repeating those last two sentences?"

"What? That I want you in my life? That's nothing new. Haven't you known that all along?" He sounded almost annoyed. "Anyway, I too will be working my ass off. And I will see you every weekend when I fly back to Fairbanks to keep the trucking company afloat."

"I thought Alaska Truck Transport was a joint project with The Bering Strait Natives?" I asked, buying time while trying to control my emotions . . . had I just heard him make a commitment? It sure sounded like it! I kept my voice even, hiding my excitement. "Why can't BSN look after it? I would rather come to Hawaii with you."

"I'd love that, honey, but there's no job for you there and I won't have time to do anything but work. As for BSN, I've bought out their half of ATT."

"Oh God, Doug. Yes, I want to see you. I . . . I think I love you." I stumbled over the words. "But I would have to sell my houseboat, cancel my television show . . . Do you love me? You've never said so."

"Of course I do, sweetheart. So let's do it! Cancel the show . . . but keep the boat. We can use it for vacations."

I hung up the phone in a daze. Did that all just happen? And I said I loved him. Did I really? Or was I talking myself into it so I could bring Benny home? It was all so sudden that I couldn't think straight. Questions tumbled over each other. How long would his divorce take? Were we really in love? Would I be happy living in Alaska? Could I manage a trucking company, for God's sake!? I frowned.

Five minutes later, the phone rang again. I snatched up the receiver.

"You can pick up your ticket from the American Airlines counter in Miami," he said without preamble. "You will fly out next Monday."

"So soon?" I felt the panic rising.

"The sooner the better. I don't want you changing your mind." The connection was cut; he must have hung up. I collapsed onto the sofa. This was too much. I couldn't think. Again the phone rang. Trembling now, I lifted it once more.

"Baby. This is all so sudden," I said. "Couldn't I have a little more time to think?"

"Think about what? And sure it was sudden. How did you know?"

"What, what?" More confused than ever, I recognized Brooke's voice.

"Who told you we got married? It only happened last night."

"Brooke. Please take it from the top. I'm a little hazy at the moment."

"You sure are, kiddo. Well, aren't you gonna congratulate me? David and I tied the knot last night. You can call me Mrs. David Holmes."

"Well, congratulations. Why wasn't I invited to the wedding? Where are you?" Life was just becoming too confusing altogether.

"In Vegas, stupid. And we invited no one. Elvis married us in a little chapel with Elvis's family as witnesses."

"This has been some day. When are you coming back? I'd like to see you before I go."

"Next week. Go where?"

"To Alaska. I'm gonna manage Doug's trucking company and I think we're getting married."

"What!?" she screamed, forcing me to move the receiver away from my ear. "Are you bloody nuts?"

CHAPTER 33

Out Of My Comfort Zone

Doug was waiting for me at the Anchorage airport and my heart quickened at the sight of him standing there. I ran towards him, expecting a long hug and a kiss. It was a shock when he smiled stiffly and shook my hand. He was as welcoming as that monstrous polar bear which still stood in its glass container, mutely menacing the travelers. What am I doing here, I wondered?

I followed Doug as he bustled ahead, clearing a way through the multitude of hulking, work-clothed men who seemed to always clog the Anchorage airport. Since Alyeska's pipeline construction had started, thousands of workers had flooded into Alaska, turning Anchorage, Fairbanks and Valdez into boomtowns.

We thrust onwards towards the Air Alaska counter to change to a smaller plane and continue onto Fairbanks.

"Go get us a coffee while I attend to our boarding passes," Doug commanded, his chauvinism rising to the occasion. "There's a table with free coffee-makings on the other side of the passenger lounge." He waved his hand in the direction.

I nervously obeyed and, while carrying the cardboard cup back, spilt some of the hot brew along the way. Doug was talking to a couple of rugged-looking, unshaven individuals in coveralls as I approached. Doug was dressed in gray trousers and a sports jacket, looking reasonably well-groomed. Beardless, and with a decent haircut, he stood out from the crowd.

The pair jerked to attention when I joined them.

"Here, meet June," Doug said. "She is my newest Fairbanks employee."

They looked surprised. "Gonna work in the office is she?" one grinned before pointedly adding, "How's Jean doing?"

"I'm sure she's fine and, no, June is my new dispatcher."

I couldn't miss the raised eyebrows and I was glad when they left to take a flight to Prudhoe. Soon thereafter, our own boarding call echoed throughout the busy airport and we were on our way.

During the short flight, I suffered a few misgivings about this huge new step. Doug seemed so remote. Had I annoyed him somehow? Had he changed his mind about us? Or was his formality due to being seen in public with me before his divorce was final? I hoped that was the answer.

Waiting for us at the small Fairbanks airport was a young, blonde man with a beer belly straining the buttons of his checked shirt. He was wearing the peculiar rubber boots that so many Alaskan men wore and, which I would later learn were called 'Bunny Boots'. Doug introduced him as Bob. The man frowned and greeted me coolly. I was soon forgotten as the men fell into conversation while heading for the parking lot. The unpaved lot was filled with four-wheel drive vehicles and the men stopped before a brown, two-tone Jeep Cherokee with an ATT logo on the door.

"Do you want me to drive?" Bob asked.

"Sure." Doug turned and opened the back door for me. As he helped me in, he squeezed my hand. It was the first glimmer of affection since my arrival and I held back tears, feeling completely lost, ignored and out of my comfort zone.

"When do you head back to Idaho?" Doug asked Bob after we drove off.

"Later today! I was just waiting for you to get here."

"Did you find me an apartment?" Doug asked.

"No. The lease wasn't up on mine so I thought you could take that over. It's close to the truck yard and has two bedrooms. Besides, the lease still has eight months to run at the old rent. Since all these yobos have started arriving from the lower forty-eight, the price of housing has tripled along with everything else, including crime."

"Your apartment will work fine. I might have to use it for June; she's going to be doing the dispatching. I have to go to Hawaii. Your leaving has left me in a bit of a bind."

"I'm sorry, Doug. Our baby is due any day. If I don't get back, my wife will divorce me. Who's my replacement, did you say?"

"June."

"I don't think I know him."

"Her, not him . . . in the back seat. June. You just met."

I thought I heard the man splutter, the sound increasing my foreboding.

We were passing through a small, nondescript town of rambling one and two-story dusty, brown buildings. There were no modern, glass skyscrapers in Fairbanks. Before long, we left the hard-top road and bumped along over a dirt surface. I pondered the color of the dirt—a whitish yellow! I wondered why I always noticed such things; yellow dust, white dust, red dust, black dust. Abstract thoughts! Then I thought of Bob's words: 'crime had tripled.'

"What's the law around these parts on carrying a firearm?" I asked.

"Everyone has one. We're the hunting capital of the world," Bob boasted.

"You can carry or wear one as long as it's visible," Doug added. "Why do you ask?"

"Oh, no reason." I wasn't planning to stay alone and unprotected in a strange boomtown filled with yobos.

We passed a few substantial log buildings. Caribou horns decorated the doorways, looking more like the Alaska I had expected. Then, on the very outskirts of town, I saw a cluster of multi-story, red brick buildings; the signs out front proclaiming them as The Fairbanks University. At least it would have a library, I thought, and probably some sporting facilities. Maybe it would even have a swimming pool. This could be a good opportunity to take classes and improve my faltering Japanese. I filed it away for future reference,

Fields of green next came into view. I recognized giant-size vegetables sprouting from the ground. One field was dotted with huge golden mounds which looked strong enough for a man to sit upon. I couldn't believe they were pumpkins and I interrupted the men's conversation to question them about it.

"We get sun twenty-four-seven during summer," Doug explained. "Great for growing mammoth veggies."

"And mosquitos," Bob added. "The world's largest."

Moments later, we passed through a set of large, double gates, into an untidy yard surrounded by high, galvanized-wire fencing. Two monster trucks stood side by side, one with its hood unfolded. A few flatbeds sat nearby and alongside the fence was a sprawling heap of tires. Bob brought the Jeep to a halt between a long, silver cylindrical trailer and a larger, bulkier tank trailer which was hitched onto a truck displaying the word 'Kenworth'. The engine was purring, the driver's side door hung open; but no driver was in sight.

"Do you know who's taking this load?" Doug asked Bob.

"Joe, the guy from Montana. He's our best driver but you gotta watch the son-of-a-bitch. He's a scammer with the time sheets."

With my anxiety level reaching new heights, I inhaled diesel fumes while following the two men across the gravel-strewn ground towards a metal warehouse-style shed. We passed through the cavernous opening, and inside, two grease-stained men in dark coveralls were bent over a couple of truck engines. A short, muscular man wearing a baseball cap stood talking to them. He held a cup of steaming coffee and its pleasing aroma mingled with the less inviting odors of grease, diesel and dust. The men stopped what they were doing as we entered. Forgoing any greeting, Doug asked, "What's wrong with number eight?" indicating the truck one of them was working on.

A thin, older mechanic finished wiping his hands on a blackened cloth, then answered, "She's been overheating. I've just replaced the water pump."

I stared around, growing more nervous by the minute. Doug was going to take off and leave me to run this? What had I been thinking?

"And you must be Joe, right?" Doug turned his gaze to the man with the coffee.

"Right on, buddy."

"I'm not your buddy, I'm your boss. Doug Lantz is the name." He pulled me forward. "And this is June. She is going to replace Bob as your new dispatcher."

The man choked on the coffee and the two mechanics frowned.

"Like hell she is!" blurted Joe. "I don't take no orders from no goddamn woman."

"Then climb on the first plane back to Montana," Doug growled.

"Aw, Doug. There ain't no female dispatchers in Alaska. If we have to take orders from a woman, we'll be a laughingstock amongst the other drivers."

"I know one other company with a female dispatcher."

"Yeah! But she's the owner."

"I'm not here to argue with you. As of next week, June's your boss. Now if you want to work here, put that goddamn drink down and haul ass. That truck is burning gas on my penny and time is money."

I watched the driver throw the dregs of his drink on the ground and follow it with an angry spit. He spun on his heel then loped angrily to his truck. I fought a wave of absolute disbelief. Doug was leaving me to run this business after only one week? Was the man crazy? Was I?

I followed Doug and his dispatcher into a back office. It smelled exactly like the workshop. The desk top was lost beneath a mountain of grease-smeared books, invoices, miscellaneous papers and a dented oil can. I could not envision myself in this new domain. After Bob finished bringing Doug up to date, he asked if one of the mechanics could drive him to the airport. Before leaving, he turned to Doug and in a loud voice—for my benefit, I thought—he said, "I hope you don't mind Doug. While I'm in Anchorage, I want to drop by and say goodbye to Jean. Your wife has been like a second mother to me."

An hour later, Doug closed the office door. We were alone at last.

"Now come here, woman." He said, grabbing me and pulling me against his chest. I surprised us both by bursting into tears.

CHAPTER 34

Fairbanks

It was early morning of my fourth day in Fairbanks. Or so I thought. I could never tell what time of the night or day it was with the blasted sun shining all the time. I turned over in the narrow single bed. Doug was still asleep in the identical bed on the opposite side of the room. I scowled at the cheap, veneer wood that lined the unadorned walls. It smelled of formaldehyde. A bare light bulb hung on a black wire from the center of the ceiling.

How I longed for my leopard-skin tent with its mirrors, its cushions, its palms and spears. How I longed for the floor to roll beneath my feet and the sweet perfume of ocean water to cleanse my nostrils, which at that moment, felt blocked. The air was so dry. Surely I couldn't go ahead with this? But what options did I have if I needed a marriage partner to bring Benny to the U.S.? The previous night, Doug had assured me he wanted the child as much as I did. What he really meant, I was sure, was that he wanted me as much as I wanted the child. He remained undemonstrative but those gray eyes betrayed him. I felt certain he had fallen hard. After a couple of drinks, he was prone to repeat "I have never met a woman quite like you."

I cared more for him at such times when he seemed to soften and become vulnerable. After re-assessing the sacrifice I was making, I tried harder to analyse my feelings. I loved Doug's intelligence, his ruggedness. However, I was not blinded by love and since arriving in Fairbanks, I had discovered a brusque side of him that I didn't like. He was embarrassingly rude to some of his drivers and he could quickly fly into a rage. When I complained about the way he had spoken to one of the men, he growled, "I don't trust that asshole. I know how long it takes to get up there, unload and get back. He's consistently late and always has a lame excuse. Every extra hour for that fucker is profit out of our pockets. $50,000-$60,000 a year! I drove trucks for years over the Alcan in the middle of winter. No fuckin' truck driver is worth $50,000!"

"Well, if that's what they're paid here, losing your temper won't help," I had admonished.

Now I stared at him as he slept. He was still an enigma to me. He could change from class to crass and back in an instant. I recalled the end of that conversation about the drivers.

"They'll give you hell when I leave," he had warned me. "They'll test you every step of the way. Don't let them fool you. You've got to anticipate their every move."

I wondered exactly how I was meant to anticipate things I had no experience with. Doug's bed creaked as he moved and I heard him yawn loudly.

"Good morning, babe," he mumbled. I climbed out of bed, padded across the linoleum barefooted and squeezed in beside him.

"Good morning, Dougie." I knew he hated that handle but I laughed and kissed him before he could complain. He wrapped one arm around me, cupping my breast in his hand.

"I've been lying here worrying if I can handle this job when you go," I said. "Did your wife ever help in the business?"

"Jean? Good heavens, no. Anyone could walk all over her. A pathetic, weak woman. She's the opposite of you; that's why I love you. Besides, Jean's had a serious drinking problem for years. I don't know how I've hung in there this long. Pity, I suppose. She's not a bad person."

We fell silent and I contemplated his words, particularly the 'not a bad person' part. At times, I felt a twinge of guilt but they were fleeting. With or without me, they had been heading for divorce.

Doug slapped me over the behind. "Time to rise and shine, honey! There's work waiting."

I stared up at the light tumbling in through the top half of the window where the tinfoil had come unstuck and fallen down. I'd noticed several houses in Fairbanks had tinfoil-covered windows and I made a mental note to mail-order for some black-out blinds.

"Oh, alright," I replied petulantly. "But I have a question, Doug. This apartment is pretty nasty. Do you think I could spend a bit of money to make it more livable?"

"Don't try to replace your houseboat here. But I will set up a bank account for you. Please don't go overboard. This is only a rental you know." He stretched before pushing me out of bed.

The dreaded day had arrived. Doug was leaving for Hawaii where his vessel, newly-registered as The Alaska Gulf, was in dry dock. Modifications would turn her from a water tanker into a mud carrier. During the previous week, as part of my intensive learning, I had viewed the drilling-mud when the men loaded it into the tankers; it was not really a mud at all but actually a loose powder.

Time had flown by with so much to absorb. I had taken a phone call from Canadian Pacific Railways telling me that a new rail car had arrived. I drove the Jeep, following the trucks over to the siding where I watched the unloading of the 'mud'. Huge, wide-mouthed hoses were attached between an outlet on the top of the train tank to the outlet on ATT's truck tankers. After each end was coupled, powerful, motorized blowers blew the powder from one tank into the other. This took considerable time and our entire fleet of trucks did not entirely empty the rail car. It would remain on the siding, repeatedly filling the trucks as they returned from up north. By the time the rail car was empty, another would have arrived to take its place.

My job was to keep the rail cars coming and keep the trucks running on schedule. Schedule meant each driver made two trips a week and was back in the yard no later than midnight on Fridays. The most economical way to run the business was to stagger the return of the drivers so that the trucks weren't all lined up together as that wasted time and company money while drivers stood around smoking, waiting their turn. Of course, the same thing applied to the unloading when they arrived in Prudhoe Bay but I had no control over that end. Several other trucking companies hauled the same product so if the unloading line was long, there was nothing the drivers could do but wait their turn and snatch a few hours of needed sleep.

Fortunately, my job did not involve the two mechanics; Doug and they communicated via phone each day.

A round trip to Prudhoe Bay was almost a thousand miles. I was told that the mountainous roads were the devil's own course. Keeping the trucks running was an expensive and full-time job, even though most were quite new, having been recently purchased from Kenworth in Seattle.

The notorious Teamsters Union had an iron grip on all Alaskan trucking companies. If the drivers did not arrive back by midnight Friday, they went onto double-time. By Sunday, they were on triple-time.

A breakdown out in that wilderness meant disaster. Not only was the company paying penalty time to the driver but getting a mechanic and the correct parts out to the truck were a logistical nightmare. The mechanics had to rely on the driver's assessment of the problem to determine which parts were needed. If the truck couldn't be fixed on the road and had to be towed back, that meant two trucks losing revenue. Clearly, keeping the machinery in tiptop condition was imperative and I understood why Doug handled his mechanics with great care. I was awed by the responsibility he had given me and surprised at his trust.

CHAPTER 35

From T.V Host To Truck Dispatcher

I enjoy human interaction but I also enjoy my own company and seldom feel lonely. It's a matter of keeping busy, doing what you enjoy, and maintaining balance. Those first few months in Alaska were an exception. I was so lonely and I certainly wasn't doing something I enjoyed. I was imbalanced to the point of almost becoming unbalanced. Most of the drivers hated my guts and I had no one to talk to. I got along fine with the mechanics and the two young Inuit apprentices but we had nothing in common.

About once a week I called Brooke. She was always good for a laugh but as she boasted about her trips to Monaco, her five-star hotel stays, and her recently acquired race horses, I hung up feeling more depressed.

I sat in the office, recalling the last time I had felt so lonely. It had been a Christmas Day, ten years earlier in Kobe, Japan. The picture was firmly entrenched in the recesses of my mind.

I remembered sitting alone in a steak house, eating one of those tender pieces of meat that made Kobe famous. As I watched a happy Japanese family at the next table, the juicy steak tasted like sawdust in my mouth. That was one of the rare times when I longed to stop traveling and return to my family in Australia. I remembered the lump that had risen in my throat and how I hurried out of the restaurant, unable to finish my meal.

Now, sitting behind the battered desk, staring at a tangle of radiator belts hanging from a nail in the wall, that awful sense of loneliness was engulfing me once more. When the cumbersome black phone rang, I snatched it up.

"Hullo. Hullo," I blabbed.

"Hullo yourself. It's me, checking up on how everything's going?" Doug sounded worried.

"You said you would be back every weekend. Why weren't you?"

"I had to hire the workers this week and it's too soon to leave them. We're working around the clock. Next weekend, I'll be there for sure."

"Don't make empty promises, Doug. These drivers are giving me a hard time like you predicted." My voice began rising. "They hate my guts, all except the mechanics and your two Alaskan gypo drivers."

"Don't take it personally, Junie Moon. They just hate taking orders from a woman. What have they done now?"

"Well, Joe said he had a breakdown on Friday night. He didn't come in until Saturday afternoon. I wouldn't have been angry but then one of the Alaskan drivers said he passed Joe's truck parked at an Alyeska camp. Apparently he has a girl friend there. So the bastard spent the night with his girlfriend while we're paying him by the hour. What can I do?

"We can't fire the son-of-a-bitch. Not without the Teamsters coming down on us like a ton of bricks. Besides, he's our best driver. Look, next Monday morning you hold him back. Say you can't let the truck go out again until the mechanics have given it a thorough overhaul. Make him miss the first trip so he only goes out on Wednesday. We'll lose money but it might teach him a lesson."

"Okay, I'll give it a try." I sighed heavily. "Just make sure you're back here next weekend. It's beginning to get cold and I desperately need a warm snuggle."

After cradling the phone, I picked up the small, framed photo of Ben. It was a blow-up of his passport picture which had been taken the previous month. I had celebrated, that joyous day, when I learned he had that document . . . one step closer in the long, slow process. Ben looked bright-eyed and happy in the photo. I stared at it hard but it did not bring quite the pleasure it usually did.

"I hope you're worth this, little boy," I said.

Doug did return the next weekend and we had our first date.

"What would you like to do?" he asked.

"I don't know. There's nowhere much to go around here unless you're into hunting and fishing . . ."

"How about we go for a drive out into the country for a picnic? I know a nice place where there is an old, disused gold mine. The autumn leaves will be lovely this time of the year."

And so our first date was spent looking at some rusting equipment in a hollow, about twenty-five miles outside of Fairbanks. But he was right about the beautiful fiery backdrop of orange, yellow and red leaves. That rugged man was as enigmatic as ever.

Weeks passed. I was handling the job okay but not entirely worry-free. Doug returned to Fairbanks two weekends each month and I spent one weekend each month in Hawaii. It was not as romantic as it sounds. At first, he had been living in a hotel close to the docks. However, as the workload became heavier, he checked out of the hotel and we slept aboard the vessel which was a hive of activity day and night. Welders, electricians and miscellaneous workers scrambled all over the place. My visits did not stop Doug from working. If he wasn't too tired at night, we changed into clean clothes and went ashore for dinner.

It was rough living in his small captain's quarters. Against one wall, sitting high off the floor was a bunk built of beautiful timber. It was so narrow that the two of us, even lying sideways in spoon-fashion, could barely fit into it. The entire ship was dusty, covered in gritty metal shavings. Hoses and wires covered the passageways in a profuse, tangled mess, constantly tripping me up. Every few yards, I had to pass helmeted welders; their cutting torches spraying me with flying sparks and hot metal chips. The large galley was not yet up and running. I cooked our lunch crouched over a portable gas burner, shielded from the wind in one of the narrow passageways. As I compared it to all the lesser moments of my life, it was an experience!

The boat was out of dry dock and sat in the water at a shipyard. On one of my visits, Doug seemed particularly frantic at the innumerable delays plaguing the work.

"That truck should have been here an hour ago! Everyone's on damn 'manana' time out here," he complained, glancing angrily at his gold-nugget watch. "The dock workers leave at five sharp so there will be no one to work the hydraulics and lower the platform. How the hell can we get the friggin' truck on deck to unload it today? The men need that steel to keep on working!"

Doug kept checking his watch, becoming more infuriated by the minute. He had begged the workers to wait for the arrival of the truck to no avail. Quitting time came. Our night crew arrived moments before the dockhands raised the ramp and left. The bridge to land was no longer horizontal but towered vertically from the dock's edge.

At five-thirty, a small truck pulled up on shore adjacent to the ship.

"What the hell took you so long?" Doug shouted across at the driver.

"Traffic jam," the driver yelled back, scratching his head.

"You shoulda fuckin' started out earlier!" Doug yelled again as the driver climbed out of the rig and went to stand on the dock's edge. "You just stay there while I work out what to do. I need that fuckin' load."

My instincts were to hide when Doug became this angry. He never took it out on me but I always felt so uncomfortable when he was being rude to people. I watched him bustling about now. He was talking to a couple of the ship's welders. They had been unable to start work without the new load of steel. One of them scurried away, and returned moments later with an armful of thick rope. Curiosity got the better of me and I picked my way through the hoses to join the men.

"What are you going to do, Doug?"

"Watch and learn, woman," he replied quickly as he and the two welders unwound the rope and threaded it through holes they had drilled in a slab of wood. Now that he had a plan, he seemed to calm down.

"Have you ever heard of a Bosun's chair?" he asked, walking to the very edge of the vessel and yelling to the truck driver to catch the rope when he threw it.

"Fasten that mother tight to a cleat," he ordered before turning back to me.

"I'm gonna try and get into that machinery shack. I'll run the damned hydraulics myself and lower that friggin' thing."

"Won't you get into trouble tomorrow?" I asked nervously.

"Who cares, the money I'm paying them."

By then, with the help of his men, he had attached two lengths of rope between the ship and shore. He climbed onto the slab of wood which resembled a child's swing and pushed off the ship into midair. Now the deck of the ship sat about fourteen feet above the water with several feet between it and dry land. Doug, looking pleased with himself, grabbed the ropes and slowly maneuvered the wooden swing along the taut ropes high above the water. He was halfway across when a fierce gust of wind blew in, pushing The Alaska Gulf ever so slowly towards shore. The ropes of the Bosun's chair went slack . . . Doug and his Bosun's chair tumbled into the water below. At first I panicked, fearing the ship would crush him but he soon surfaced, spitting, spluttering and swearing. Nobody dared laugh as his language turned the air blue while he slipped and slithered up the steep, muddy bank.

Bedraggled and wet, he made it to the top and began banging and pulling at the door of the small shack housing the hydraulics. Even insanity could not give him the strength to get it open. By that time, I had to retreat to his cabin, desperate to keep him from hearing my laughter. The men, too, were smothering little bursts of amusement.

When I returned to the deck, Doug had given up trying to break into the hydraulics shed. I watched him and the truck driver maneuver two huge planks of wood between the ship and shore. They kept stopping and measuring the distance between the two pieces before adjusting them slightly. 'What on earth is he doing now?' I wondered. Now, all the workers had come to stand on deck and stare. A small crowd of people had gathered from nowhere and were watching from the shore as well. Then it seemed as if Doug and the truck driver were having a heated argument. I couldn't quite make out what they were saying but the driver kept vehemently shaking his head. I saw him throw his arms in the air and walk away. Doug climbed into the truck and fear instantly clutched my throat.

"Oh no, Doug. No!" I yelled as he started up the engine. Men on both sides were wide-eyed with incredulity. Inch by inch, Doug edged that truck onto the boards and approached the water as every man and the one woman there held their breath. Sick with anxiety, I turned away, unable to look. Yet, unable not to look, I turned back in time to see him give a burst of acceleration which caused the truck to almost leap across the water before he jammed on the brakes, stopping it before it hit the far side of the ship. The onlookers roared and clapped as loud as any spectators at the Rose Bowl.

"You stupid bastard," I swore, running up to him, filled with a mix of anger and pride as he climbed out of the truck.

"I told you I'd do it somehow," he said proudly, pushing me aside as he organized the unloading.

CHAPTER 36

Alaskans Celebrate Australia Day

Months passed, and back in Fairbanks, we were well into the darkness of winter. The mechanics fitted chains to the Jeep's tires but still I had trouble driving over the ice. More than once, I slid off the road into a gully, mortified at having to call the truck yard and ask them to send a tractor to pull me out. The men loved my mistakes which re-enforced their sense of superiority. I regularly came close to quitting, frustrated by the work, the winter weather, and the slow progress of Doug's divorce. His wife was determined to leave him penniless. Meanwhile, I continued sending little care packages to the orphanage in Kerala, India. I had three choices: Give up on adoption; marry Doug and get home-study/immigration approval for Benny; or go alone and live in India. Looking back, it's hard to believe how times have changed. Not only can single people adopt nowadays but so can couples living in homosexual relationships.

I battled on at the truck yard, however the challenges of gaining the drivers' respect, seemed insurmountable as I continued making mistakes.

Each truck had a large, black vinyl identifying number attached to the driver's side window. One had fallen off and I rushed out early one morning to replace it before the driver left. Even wearing woolen gloves, I could feel the cold of the metal rungs as I climbed up the truck's ladder. I clutched the new number and a pair of scissors in one hand, ready to scrape the remnants of the old number off the glass. My leather-soled boots kept slipping on the icy rungs. Fearful of falling, I freed up both hands by sticking the scissors in my mouth. Minutes later when I tried to remove them, they were stuck firm. Panicking, I tugged hard enough to bring tears to my eyes. No success. I yelled in alarm and the men came running. With my tongue and my mouth cemented firmly to the steel, I yanked with super-human strength. The scissors flew free, taking a chunk of my tongue and lip with them. I howled in pain while the audience laughed so hard that a few collapsed into the snow.

"Cheechako, Cheechako!" the Inuit apprentices screamed, holding their sides and rolling their eyes. Later that night when I asked Doug over the phone what it meant, he answered, "Greenhorn. Why, where did you hear that?"

"Oh, never mind." I said.

I had decorated the apartment almost immediately after arriving in Fairbanks. I knew winter would bring with it a totally white landscape so I had given my new home some splashes of green.

I must have bought a hundred trailing plants and hung them from every square foot of living room ceiling space. Purple grow-lights nurtured them and soon those babies were trailing foliage, vines reaching the floor.

When winter arrived, I combated the dry Alaskan air by adding humidity, continually boiling water in huge cauldrons on the gas stove. The consequences of all this was an artificially-created, steaming jungle. Still not satisfied, I added a floor-to-ceiling aviary in one corner.

In Australia, I grew up surrounded by beautiful, colored parrots which I missed terribly. Keeping my new flock happy, I dragged a dead tree into their cage. Bathing facilities were implemented by installing an artificial rock waterfall.

After throwing hay on the floor of the enclosure, I purchased a rabbit and named it Cedric. Its namesake was a prop I had used while working in Vietnam as a magician's assistant. The new Cedric kept hopping, dodging missiles from above. Shit happens!

It was heavenly to come home from a hard day's work and relax to the sounds of running water and tumultuous birdsong. Unfortunately, like me, my feathered friends could not determine night from day. By the arrival of winter, some had already perished from strained vocal cords.

Late for work one morning, I rushed into the living room and couldn't open the door. The wind was howling outside but, inside, the apartment was nice and steamy warm. The veneered wood walls streamed with water rivulets from the bubbling cauldrons. Steam had turned the windows white and the wet birds screeched cheerfully while shaking out their feathers.

I yanked the door again to no avail; it was one big sheet of ice. Time was wasting and I had trucks to get on the road. Running through the vines, I pulled open a kitchen drawer and dragged out a carving knife. For the next fifteen minutes, I chipped frantically but made no headway. I gradually realized my predicament was caused by the freezing wind which had blown in through the cracks around the door, turning the water into ice. Running through the jungle once more, I hoisted a heavy pot of boiling water from the stove. Panting from the weight, I hurled it against the frozen door. Some of it remained there, adding further ice, but most ran to the square slab of linoleum at the foot of the door transforming that into a skating rink. Chip—slip—fall! Chip—slip—fall! I hate to quit but I knew when I was beaten; I phoned the yard and asked for help. The mechanics tried to show respect but I did hear strangled laughter as they suggested I use a hair dryer.

I had heard about cabin fever and how a lot of the native people, suffering that affliction, got drunk throughout winter. With the after-Christmas letdown, I could well relate, and was back on the sleeping pills. January approached and, with it, Australia Day, which was celebrated every year on the 26th of the month. I decided to break out of the doldrums with a party. If only I had friends to invite! That problem was solved by placing an advertisement in the Fairbanks newspaper. The advert read: 'Any Aussies, Kiwis, friends of Down Under, or those with an interest in Australia, please gather at The Fox Tavern on the 26th to celebrate Australia Day.'

Doug had introduced me to the Fox Tavern during one of his visits and it quickly became my haven whenever I felt low and needed a quiet drink. At that time, Fox had a population of maybe fifty. It was hard to say for many of the elusive locals were gold miners in summer and hunters in winter; therefore, often absent. The village was located ten miles northeast of Fairbanks on the Steese Highway. It was the last outpost of civilization before heading north to Prudhoe Bay.

The tavern was the village's only significant building. Not surprisingly, it was constructed of logs adorned with the compulsory caribou horns. Its small, neon sign blinked bravely in the wilderness, welcoming weary travelers indoors to defrost around a blazing fire. Trappers and hunters could leave their bear-and-moose-laden pickups in the parking lot. Rifles rested against the bar while rugged men discussed the pros and cons of the wildlife wardens who prowled on the lookout for poachers. It was a far cry from the elegant clubs I had frequented in New York or the oceanfront places of Miami but it certainly had character.

As the 26th approached, I had written to Qantas of my intent and they kindly sent me dozens of posters of Australia. These looked good enough to tempt me home with scenes of bronzed lifesavers leaping from frothy, sunlit surf . . . of bikini-clad buxom beauties reclining on the sand . . . of kangaroos grazing in bushland or of drovers rounding up sheep among the gum trees.

Andy, the friendly manager, drooled over our Aussie girls as he lined the pub walls with the posters. "I've gotta get me down thataway some day," he drawled while hanging a large Aussie flag behind the bar.

I was amazed, when on the 26th, hundreds of people showed up. Who would have known that Australia had so many friends in Alaska? Half the Fairbanks University Faculty arrived.

Unbeknownst to me, the professor from my Japanese class had written to Buckingham Palace regarding the event. On the night of the celebration, he climbed upon the bar, yelled for silence, and read the letter from the Queen's secretary.

The roomful of drunks responded with a rousing reception and we raised our glasses in several innovative toasts to the Queen. Outside, a gale was blowing but, inside, the overheated room was abuzz with the sounds of clinking glass, occasional shattering glass, and continual discordant mutterings of 'Here's to Lizzie' . . . and bagpipes!'

These were being played by another professor who brought along his instrument and blew until he collapsed. Dancing to bagpipes is challenging—and exhausting—but we prevailed until one overly enthusiastic chap fell into the fireplace and had to be doused with beer. I think that was just before a late arrival broke the door when shooting through it on a skidoo. It was a night worthy of any good bunch of Aussies, even though none were present except me. And, of course, we had no shrimp for the 'barby' but we made do with bear.

At the end of the night, Andy commented, "You Aussies sure know how to party. I think I'll make this an annual event."

CHAPTER 37

I knew another winter was over when the mechanics removed the chains from the Jeep. What a relief! I was sick of the dark; sick of having to plug the Jeep into the outdoor electrical socket every night to prevent the engine from freezing up; sick of missing every movie climax when I had to continually leave the warmth of the theater and run out into the cold.

I was also sick of choking on ghastly fumes from car exhausts, fumes that remained trapped close to the ground by ice-fog; I could see it swirling and glinting in utter blackness whenever I switched on the car headlights.

Then later, as winter neared its end, we found ourselves in 'break-up'. This was when the ice began melting, leaving puddles everywhere and gigantic piles of mud-streaked, dirty snow along the edges of the roads. Oh, the joy.

"I have such good news!" I cried over the phone to Doug.

"Is it about the boy?"

"No. It's too soon for that. We're not married, remember?" I was instantly sorry it sounded like an accusation.

"You know the end's in sight."

I stared at a large pair of rubber boots in the corner of the office. They sat on the floor beneath a wall hook which held a rubber apron. This was essential regulation gear for the drivers whenever they unloaded acid at the rail siding. I worried about such loads, and the men who had the dangerous job of transporting them over icy roads. The acid was occasionally necessary in case a blockage occurred during the drilling.

I pulled my attention away from the apron back to the phone. 'End in sight' indeed! Belatedly, I answered Doug.

"My mother and youngest sister, Jan, are coming to visit. They have never been outside Australia. I can't wait for them to get here!"

"Well, that is exciting for you, honey. I look forward to meeting them." His words jolted me.

"What about our sleeping arrangements?" I blurted. "I won't be comfortable if Mum discovers we're sleeping together."

"Have the boys come over and put one of the beds into the second bedroom. You can all share a room while I suffer."

"Serves you right!" I laughed.

The sun was still shining when the plane dropped into the small airfield. It was 10:00 p.m. As I waited for the passengers to disembark, I hopped from foot to foot, craning my neck. Almost five years had passed since I last saw my mother. She would be almost sixty years old and I was sure she would be exhausted after such a long trip. Anxiously, I watched the stream of humanity become a trickle and there was no sign of her . . . I wondered if she had missed the plane. A huge wave of disappointment was beginning to swell when she bounced into view, followed more sedately by my teenage sister, Jan. I waved and caught their attention. They waved wildly and mum almost ran down the stairs, leaving Jan behind. We hugged and chattered excitedly. Jan caught up and we all talked at once as I led them to the Jeep.

"It's still daylight!" Mum looked at the sky, incredulous. "When do you sleep?"

We reached the apartment and, after I opened the door, they both gasped.

"What the hell is this jungle, June? I need a machete to chop my way through." Mum's outburst caused Jan to place her hand over her mouth, stifling a giggle.

The birds, upon hearing us enter, gave a raucous welcome, screeching and yelling hysterically. Their excitement galvanized the rabbit into a wild, leaping dance around the waterfall. I noticed the poor creature was drenched. The waterfall did resemble a miniature Victoria Falls. If only I could remember to buy a less powerful pump! Mum thrust vines from her face and, while plucking a few leaves from her hair, worked her way to the corner aviary where she stood and stared.

"Do you always have to go overboard, girl? I hope you don't have Tarzan stashed away somewhere."

A picture of Doug dressed in a loincloth flashed through my mind and it was not a pretty sight.

"The chlorophyll is healthy, Mum," I answered lamely.

A few days later, Doug arrived, allowing me time off to be with Jan and my mother. My mother and Doug got along very well together. Mum was only eight years older than Doug and both of them had experienced their fair share of hard work, growing up through the depression. Jan took a little longer to warm to him after hearing him swearing at the drivers.

We had done all the usual tourist things; taken the paddle wheeler down the Chena River, eaten bear, and drank in pubs with sawdust and peanut shells littering the floor beneath a sea of women's brassieres which hung from the rafters.

"I hope we are not expected to add to this collection," Mum mumbled, dubiously eyeing the offending undies in one establishment. Like most dairy farmers, she was rather conservative and Jan, her youngest child, was painfully shy. This was their first time away from Australia and I'm sure they found it quite different.

"I would enjoy this trip better if I could get some damn sleep," Mum complained in between dainty sips from her shandy. Jan and I sat beside her, quaffing down a couple of frothy beers and Jan, unused to alcohol, was beginning to look decidedly cross-eyed.

"It's those damn birds," Mum continued, determined to spoil the moment. "The poor things don't know when to sleep. Couldn't you get some quieter ones? How about finches?"

Jan added little to the conversation. She amused herself by practicing bird sounds which she interspersed with shrill giggles.

"And please, June, would you turn that noisy waterfall off when we go to bed at night?" Mum ignored Jan. "I've never had to get up to pee so often." I wiped some froth from the tip of my nose.

"Yes, Mum. I promise to turn it off. You need sleep for tomorrow. We're flying to Anchorage for a special treat."

Jan interrupted with a quavering bird tweet and I, too, ignored her.

"We're going to do some sightseeing and then—get this! I've chartered a private plane to fly us around the glaciers."

Jan gave one last piercing whistle before toppling from her stool but Mum was so excited about the upcoming event that she failed to notice.

Two days later, we took a taxi from The Captain Cook Hotel to the airfield. Alaska has more private planes per capita than any place in the world and it has always been famous for the skills of its bush pilots. The hundreds of small villages were mostly accessible only by dog sled teams, Skidoos, or planes. Mum was agog with excitement, just as she had been almost since her arrival.

We arrived at the private airfield. Thousands of planes stretched as far as the eye could see. The taxi driver, a wizened-up little native, found our toolshed-sized charter company office without too much trouble. Our pilot, upon hearing the cab, opened a sliding window and leaned out. He didn't look much older than Jan but he had probably been flying since age ten.

"Are you ready for the sights and sounds of the Columbia Glacier?" he asked. Mum nodded eagerly; Jan looked uncertain. I gave her an encouraging slap on the back.

Soon we were strapped into the small Cessna, ready for take-off.

Anchorage, located around the Cook Inlet, is surrounded by mountains. Drafts, through and around the mountains, can be quite turbulent. Before long, we were lurching up and down, our stomachs shooting up into our throats. Jan reached for the brown paper bag and began throwing up violently. It sounded ghastly and didn't smell great either but, unable to help her, we did our best to ignore it.

We circled one particular mountain peak several times and even I was beginning to wonder why. Flying dangerously close to its thick, icy crust, I could almost reach out and touch it. Certain the pilot knew what he was doing, I remained unperturbed. During my days in Vietnam, I had flown with many crazy helicopter pilots who tried to scare me with stunts such as flying beneath bridges. Mum did not appear to be sharing my lack of concern. Her initial smile of pleasure took on a frozen look as her eyes filled with terror.

Finally, she croaked, "I'm sure this is the same mountain we have circled a dozen times, pilot. Are you lost?"

"No, Ma'am," he replied with a chuckle which was cut short by another loud upchuck from Jan. "I'm trying to find where the Dall sheep are. These mountains are usually full of them but they seem to have disappeared. Now don't you worry. They're a highlight of the trip and I won't leave here until we find them."

"To hell with the Dall sheep!" my mother retorted ungraciously. "I'll buy a post card with a photo of them. Move on, pilot!"

This was so unlike my mother who was normally ultra-polite.

"Our pilot's name is Jim, Mum." I tried to nudge her good manners while opening the window to clear the stench. An onslaught of wind blew in with gale force.

"Do you have another bag?" Jan lifted her head to whisper, a string of yellowish, windblown spittle attaching itself to her cheek.

At last, we left the mountains behind and came out into still air. I glanced back at Jan. She was slumped in her seat, her body seemingly deflated as her head lolled back, eyes closed tight in a green face.

As the miles passed, the vista became increasingly spectacular. Blue water met blue sky as glorious snow-white mountains loomed along one side. I heard Mum exhale with relief and, when I looked back again, her frozen smile had melted to normal. Finally, the glacier came into view. Mum 'ooohhed and aahhed' as she snapped away with her little camera.

"Get your camera out, Jan," she ordered excitedly. "Yours takes better pictures than mine." Jan responded with a feeble moan and unhitched her camera from around her neck before limply handing it to Mum.

"You take them, Mum," she whispered.

When all the film was used, our pilot turned the small craft and headed back the way we had come. An hour later, he began to descend.

"Are we landing, pi . . . Jim?" Mum asked. "I don't see an airstrip."

Indeed. There was none. We were approaching the shore of what looked like an island wilderness.

"Coffee break!" Jim declared. "Nothing but the best for our customers. Tighten your seat belts, ladies." And he guided our little craft down onto the water.

With the engine shut off, he and I climbed down onto the struts. I balanced myself against the body of the plane while edging to the end of the strut and catapulting myself across the small expanse of water onto dry land.

"Come on, Mum," I called. "Come on, Jan. Stretch your legs." Poor Jan was too weak from tummy convulsions to jump. She waded ashore in freezing water up to her knees.

Spindly trees, stunted by permafrost, had grown almost to the water's edge leaving us a clear strip about eight feet wide where we could stand while enjoying our refreshments. Jim produced a box of colorful, iced-donuts and the largest thermos of coffee I had ever seen. Jan gazed at the bright pink donut Jim offered her then averted her eyes and shuddered. Mum took one sip of her coffee before whispering into my ear, "June. I've got to go to the toilet. I'm going to slip in behind those trees."

"Then watch out for brown bears," I teased.

"What?" A look of horror crossed her face. "Bears! I'm not going."

"It was a joke, Mum. Come on."

But that was that, better destroyed kidneys than an encounter with a bear. She tossed her remaining coffee onto the ground; the morning tea was a bit of a washout despite Jim's best efforts. For the remainder of the journey, Mum looked agonized and kept her legs tightly crossed. I tried to hide my irritation at her constant queries of "How much further, pilot?"

Nevertheless, she spent the next twenty years telling anyone who would listen about 'the best holiday of her life'. The highlight, of course, being the trip to the glaciers.

Back in Fairbanks, just before Mum and Jan left for home, my mother pulled me aside.

"I wish you'd think twice about these adoption plans, June," she said, her sharp brown eyes penetrating through to the back of my head. "You've had a good life and it hurts me to see you throwing it all away to live like this. You don't know anything about the background of foreign, unwanted children. I've bred cows and it's all in the genes. Believe me, you could be adopting a future murderer."

"Aw, come on, Mum." I shrugged, having heard this before. "Genes aren't the whole picture. Environment and teaching play a part, too. You've never seen these poor little children the way I have."

"Well, I can tell you this. When you've got kids, you've got trouble." Her expression was so pained that I leaned forward and hugged her.

"Oh! One last thing." She shook herself free from my arms. "You can put your bed back in Doug's room now."

CHAPTER 38

Hauling A Load To Prudhoe Bay

I drove the Jeep along the now familiar road to the truck yard. Switching radio stations, I stopped at one playing 'Hits of Yesterday'. Aretha Franklin was belting out 'Chain of Fools.' My Filipino band used to play that one in Vietnam but any one of those sixties songs transported me back to the war.

The troubled dreams were rare nowadays but somehow the music—or the sound of a helicopter overhead—still filled me with an odd sense of loss. I couldn't quite explain that feeling but it was always there, lurking just below the surface, always under my skin. I pulled into the truck yard, parked the Jeep and sat awhile, not turning the engine off until the last note of Aretha faded away and my eyes were dry.

How quickly time had passed. It seemed like only yesterday that I had left Vietnam. How troubled I had been and how fast-paced my life had remained for several years. By comparison, it was now boringly normal. Or was it?

In show business, we had always referred to 'normal' people as 'straight'. In Vietnam, we had referred to those normal people as civilians. Yet, over there, I never thought of myself as a 'civilian'. I thought of myself as one of the soldiers and, in a way, I was.

I glanced out the Jeep window at the heap of old tires in front of me, the unhitched trailer beside me, and sighed deeply. *I guess I am finally normal*, I thought, reaching for the door handle. *Well, sort of.*

The phone was ringing when I entered the shed. I waved at the mechanics as I rushed past into the office. It was Doug, sounding as excited as I had ever heard him.

"It's finally all coming together, honey!" he said. "I'll be over next week for the divorce hearing. When it's over, we'll go out and celebrate. At last, I'll be a free man."

"About time!" I exulted. "But you won't be free for long. We have to get married quickly so we can get Benny."

"Of course! Now listen. While I'm in Fairbanks, I'm gonna take care of those Teamster bastards for you."

"How's that?"

"I'll tell you when I get there."

"Gee, Doug. I'm so happy! I love you, baby."

"Me, too!" he said before hanging up.

Ten days later, Doug was as good as his word. The men looked stunned when they saw him at the railway siding, filling a load.

"Whose load is that?" Joe asked as they waited their turn.

"Mine," Doug boasted. "I'll show you young studs how we Alaskans do it."

"Aw, come on, old man. You're not serious?"

"You bet I am. And when I beat you back you can eat those 'old man' words. I'll even give you a head start. We'll see who's worth their money."

After I dispatched the last driver, Doug said, "Well, come on. Hop in."

"What, me? Do you think I'm crazy? You said we were going to celebrate your divorce. This is not my idea of a celebration."

"Our celebration is on hold. You're not needed here until the drivers get back and I'll get us back ahead of them."

"For God's sake, Doug! That damned trip is not my idea of a drive through the park."

"Are we a team or not? I need you to keep me from getting tired. Come on, help me, honey."

"Damn! Wait while I grab some food and a few candies. And we'll need a flask of coffee."

Before long, I was sitting high in the cab, watching the terrain begin to climb steeply. I looked at the narrow, sparsely-graveled road. We approached the first road sign—a metal, yellow, diamond-shape. Where it had once warned 'HILL', someone—presumably one of the drivers—had scratched out the letter 'I' altering the word to 'HELL.'

"Damn! I knew I should have stayed home," I said as Doug changed gears on the noisy monster. Gravel spurted from under the wheels and we labored over our first mountain where I made the mistake of looking out the side window. I saw no ground, only a sheer drop to a canyon hundreds of feet below. That was when I began to shake.

Now the one thing in life about which I am cowardly is height. I can fly in any type of aircraft, no matter how big or small, no matter how acrobatic. But when it comes to tall things attached to the earth, I am finished. I can't cross a high bridge without my hands sweating and my heartbeat accelerating, which was exactly what was happening at that moment.

"You're not hot, are you?" Doug asked. "Do you want me to turn down the heat? You're sweating."

"Just keep your eyes on the road," I grated.

"Righto. Just pour me a coffee."

"Like hell. You keep both hands on the wheel."

He started to laugh. "I don't believe it," he said. "I've found your weakness. You're scared of heights, aren't you?"

I wiped my forehead on the sleeve of my muskrat parka and tried to quell the queasiness in my stomach.

"Yes, I'm scared, goddamnit! I don't know any other stupid woman who would make this trip."

We traveled on in silence, up one 'hill' and down another. I no longer dared to look out the window, doubting there were more than a few inches of ground between the tires and the drop off into space on my side of the road.

The CB occasionally blared to life as Doug tried to learn how far ahead his drivers were. In between times, he played classical music.

"Can't we have a bit of country and western?" I begged.

"You know I hate that rubbish. Try to cultivate a little classical appreciation," he replied, turning Bach up louder.

I shifted uncomfortably in my seat and stared straight ahead at the unchanging scenery; nothing for endless miles but snow-covered mountains and spindly white trees stunted from permafrost. Not a soul—not another truck—not a building— not even a fence! We passed the occasional bear or moose but they no longer aroused my curiosity.

After traveling for several hours, hunger pangs began competing with the fear gripping my stomach.

"When can we stop for a sandwich?" I asked.

"Don't be crazy, woman. We haven't overtaken the other drivers yet. Just pass me one." He held out his manicured hand. I gazed at the slender fingers, the tapered nails. This man was still an enigma to me. I knew no other man who cared for his hands so meticulously. He used hand-cream by the gallon and wore gloves constantly.

"Like hell, Doug. You can go hungry until this damned thing comes to a standstill."

He grumbled so I compromised and broke a sandwich into pieces, hand-feeding it into his mouth. There was no way I would let him take his hands off the wheel.

An hour later, we came upon our first truck . . . several in fact. They were clinging to the side of a soaring mountain while a helicopter hovered low overhead. Doug pulled on the noisy Jake brake and we glided downhill, edging in behind the long line of stationery vehicles. Anxious voices crackled through the cab as he turned up the CB volume. I peered ahead, trying to make sense of the bedlam.

"What is it?"

"Truck over the edge. They're air evac-ing the driver out now."

"Shit! I told you this was a bad idea." My voice rose in pitch.

"Relax, woman. No need to get your bowels in an uproar."

"Well, I think I'm about to throw up. Can we turn around now and go back?"

"Of course not! They'll have the road cleared soon. Once we cross this, the worst is behind us. Alyeska keeps a tractor here for emergencies. When the trucks are overloaded and can't make the climb, the tractor helps pull them across."

"If you say so. Anyway, we've stopped now. I'll pour you some coffee and you can grab a sandwich."

"This is a stroke of luck," he replied, disregarding the plight of the bloodied driver being airlifted into the hovering chopper. "We've caught up to those bastards now so I can pass them once we get out of here."

By the time we returned to the truck yard the next day, I had seen my fill of sheer mountain drops. I climbed stiffly from the cab.

"I'd like to stay and see those young studs eat crow when they pull in later but I'm too goddamn tired," Doug said, heading towards the Jeep. "Let's go home and have a cup of tea."

It didn't take long to reach the apartment. My Mukluks made crunching sounds as I wearily trudged across the ice ahead of Doug, who had stopped long enough to plug in the Jeep. I unlocked the front door.

"I've never been so glad to see this dump."

"Yeah. I need some zzzeee's," Doug replied, catching up. "I'm beat!"

I dashed to the toilet but minutes later, I yelled, "bloody hell!"

"What's up?" Doug called back.

"The water in the toilet bowl had turned to a block of ice. I can't flush. The damn pipes have frozen up again,"

"Goddamnit! I told those men to re-tape the pipes. Let me get a blow torch."

"Be it ever so humble," I sang off-key. "There's no place like home."

CHAPTER 39

Mexico

Brooke offered to pay for our wedding as a gift from her and David. I accepted eagerly. After all, it was thanks to me that she was now an extremely wealthy woman. Besides, Doug had told me that between his wife's substantial divorce settlement and the extra time the ship was taking to finish, he was now in a financial bind.

"Where would you like to go?" Brooke asked over the phone.

"Any place that's warm! Doug loves Hawaii. He had a condo on Maui but his wife got it in the settlement."

"How does Mexico sound? I've just heard about a fab new resort that has recently opened."

"Sounds good to me. Let me check with Doug, though I'm sure he will agree."

Some weeks later, Doug and I changed planes at the Los Angeles terminal. After meeting up with Brooke and David inside The Sports Bar, we planned to travel on together to Guadalajara on Aero Mexico.

"There there they are." I cried, spotting them and running on ahead.

"Hi, guys." I gave them each a hug. "This is exciting, isn't it?"

"Yeah! I wonder what the poor people are doing?" That had become Brooke's catch phrase since marrying David. I cringed. Obviously, she had forgotten her own 'poor people' days quickly. Since their marriage, David had been coerced into selling his beloved yacht, his Ft. Lauderdale home, and disposing off his birds and monkeys. He and Brooke had moved to California and they now lived in a millionaire's enclave on a sentry-protected piece of reclaimed waterfront land called Linda Isle. It was located an hour's drive from Los Angeles.

Doug shook hands with David and pecked Brooke on the cheek.

"Aristotle of the North!" she greeted him facetiously. "We've got thirty-five minutes until we have to board. We may as well have a quick drink while we wait. Our luggage is already checked in."

"And ours was transferred through," Doug replied.

"Why are you carrying a bed pillow?" I asked Brooke.

"It's a must." She said, "Have you tried the pillows of even the best hotels lately?"

I frowned, not sure of where she was coming from.

"Here are your tickets." Brooke handed them to me. "We'll have to split up when we get on the plane."

"Couldn't you get four seats together?" I asked.

"No. David and I are traveling in first class. I hope you don't mind, you're in economy."

I felt a ripple of annoyance. After all I had done for Brooke. And I had recently read in the newspaper that David was negotiating the sale of one of his companies with R.J. Reynolds for forty seven million. It was hard to keep a genuine smile on my face. But I kept reminding myself that she was being generous by paying for the trip. Someone had once told me 'when you lose your money, you lose your power'. I felt powerless and I didn't like it.

Once aboard the plane, Doug held my hand and said, "Don't worry, baby. Our ship will come in and we won't need favors from anyone."

Nevertheless, I started off our wedding trip feeling disappointed in Brooke and angry at myself for being ungrateful.

The two days in Guadalajara passed quickly. Doug and I went sightseeing in an old-fashioned horse and buggy while Brooke and David went shopping for furnishings for their home . . . and for clothes, for jewelry, for trinkets, for cosmetics and perfumes, for medications banned by the American FDA. We met for dinner each night.

Soon it was time for the last leg of the trip. The plane to the coast was small and had no first class so Brooke and David were forced to join the 'poor people'. After arriving at the shabby, humid airport, David quickly led us outside to the waiting air-conditioned limousine.

Manzanillo, a barren little town on Mexico's east coast, was still undiscovered by tourists. Prior to the construction of Las Hadas Resort, it contained absolutely nothing other than a cluster of dusty shacks constructed of dry earth or cement. We passed by a few dilapidated stores selling corn flour, cigarettes and soft drinks. A sole gas station must have serviced the handful of ancient vehicles we saw and most of the town's citizens were out walking or riding donkeys.

The exclusive resort had been opened a mere three months earlier. It sprawled above coastal cliffs, far removed from the poverty-stricken township. The tariff would have deterred all but the well-heeled.

We bumped along over rough roads, trying not to spill the complimentary champagne that the driver had poured for us. Leaving the dirt road, we passed through an impressive, white archway. Our chauffer parked the limousine beside a fleet of identical vehicles and indicated we check in at the reception building.

After David checked us in, we squeezed into a motorized golf buggy, leaving our luggage to be delivered separately. Cars were too large to be driven inside the resort. A narrow cobweb of lanes meandered around the hill, abuzz with identical golf carts shaded by white, canvas tops. The terrain was too steep for walking by anyone less than a marathon runner; especially under the fierce sun.

We climbed until reaching a spectacular ocean view. In the distance, a lone water skier made circles in the brilliant blue water, trailed by a vee of white foam. Higher up, I saw a cluster of bungalows, their sheer white curtains billowing from them like kites in the ocean breeze. Bougainvillea grew lushly around the white walls, their color leaping out as stark as patches of blood on a snow field. As we passed the villas, I saw that each had its own individual swimming pool.

Our mood was jovial as the four of us pressed against each other. The young Mexican driver came to a halt in front of a spacious villa. The living area, open to the elements, had a breathtaking sea view. Solid white bamboo furniture with bright, floral upholstery was scattered about the tiled floor. A bowl of tropical fruit sat vividly atop a glass table, its bright reds and yellows inescapable amid the monotone of stark white everywhere. I peeped into the two attractive bedrooms and the large, luxurious bathroom.

"Who's sleeping where?" I asked.

"Pick any room you like," Brooke answered. "David and I aren't staying here. Actually, we had reserved the Honeymoon Villa for you. It's better than this one but, once we saw the pictures, we decided to keep it for ourselves and have a second honeymoon."

The smile stiffened on my face but Doug smoothly replied, "We will be just fine here." He put his arm around my waist and gave me a little squeeze.

"Then we'll leave you to it," David said. "The driver is waiting to take us to our place. Let's meet at six o'clock in the main lobby for cocktails, okay?"

Doug and I had not pre-planned our wedding but we were certain that Manzanilla must have a justice of the peace who could marry us. On the second day, we asked the resort receptionist to arrange a limousine to take us into the small town. David and Brooke eagerly accompanied us.

We passed along the dusty, main street of the impoverished settlement. Dirty-faced children and their mothers came out to look as we passed. One little girl was holding a mangy cat and she waved as we went by. I waved back.

"She reminds me of one of the little Filipina girls who first convinced me I must adopt," I said.

"You're out of your cotton-pickin' mind," Brooke said. "Whatever happened to that exciting creature who once lived on that floating home and had a ball? Has she died?"

"Same creature, same goals. Different lifestyle."

"You're totally crazy . . . and just get a look at this dump."

"Don't be so judgmental. They are nice people," David responded sharply, reminding me that he had once spent six months a year down here on his yacht before marrying Brooke.

The slick-haired driver slid the limousine against the crumbling curb in front of a large, airy building; the most dominant one in the one-street town. Its stucco was salmon pink and a row of arches opened to wind, rain and dust.

"The mayor's office. The Chief of Police, too," the driver advised proudly.

"Which one?" Doug asked.

"Same, same," he replied with a smile.

We escaped the searing heat by passing under one of the arches. Our timing was bad for we had forgotten about siesta and no one was about.

"Anyone home?" Doug yelled.

When he received no answer, we all joined in yelling and pretty soon we were laughing at no apparent thing. Ten minutes later, as we were about to leave, a stout-bellied, unshaven Mexican wandered out, pulling a suspender up over his shoulder.

"What you gringo's want?" he asked sourly, obviously having just woken up on the wrong side of the mat.

"We want to get married, "Doug answered. "Are you the mayor? Can you marry us?"

The man straightened up, thrusting his chest out importantly. "I am mayor. I Police Chief. I do matrimonia. You pay 200 pesos. What day you want?"

"How about today?" I asked. I had worn a white-embroidered cotton skirt and an off-the-shoulder peasant blouse for the big occasion. The flowers I carried had already succumbed to the heat. Brooke was wearing a Betsy Bloomingdale number and she carried a camera, ready to record the happy occasion.

"Today no good," the public official announced churlishly. "How long passport say you come Manzanilla?"

"We came yesterday, Thursday," David replied.

"No good. No good." The chief cum mayor became agitated. "You must be five day for legal matrimonia. I marry you Tuesday, ten o'clock. Okay?"

"Yes, yes," I replied quickly, just wanting to make sure he would marry us.

"We see you Tuesday. Okay!"

He emphasized the day by expectorating a large wet patch onto the ground and walking away.

"Friendly chap," Brooke snidely remarked. "Where's the romance? Las Vegas is better than this. Why don't we fly there?"

"No way," I answered. "We're here now and I'm getting married here."

"There's just one little problem," David interjected. I groaned.

"No problems, please!"

"I have to be back in Oregon on Monday for a board of directors meeting. I can't miss it. Brooke and I have to leave late Sunday."

"No problem at all." Doug came to the rescue. "I'm sure June will be disappointed that you are not here but we will just have to stay and get married by ourselves."

"Well, Brooke and I eloped and married alone," David said. "But, unfortunately, I've only reserved the villas until Sunday night."

"A minor detail," Doug said. "I'll arrange the extra two nights. You've done enough, David, and we are grateful." Doug was a proud man and I knew this situation must have pained him.

CHAPTER 40

Mexican Wedding

The day of our wedding dawned steaming hot, as usual. Doug had dressed in a cream, lightweight suit. I wore the same outfit as the first time.

"Very sorry, sir," the suave, young man at the reception desk said. "All the limousines are busy this morning. Maybe I can call a taxi to come from town and get you?"

"I'll bet they would find a limousine for David," I muttered, glaring at the concierge.

"Don't spoil our day over trivia," Doug said. He turned to the fellow and said, "That will be fine. Thank you."

Fifteen minutes later, a crumpled, red cab with no windows rattled up. Doug opened the back door; I shoved aside a few fowl feathers and climbed in.

Doug was in an exhilarated mood and he chatted with the cabbie as we traveled. It was pretty difficult with the language barrier problem but maybe the man understood for he kept taking his eyes off the narrow, winding road to turn his head, giving us a big, toothless grin.

It was 10:02 when we entered the pink building. The police chief appeared out of a small, back office looking more disheveled than on our previous visit and smelling of cheap wine.

"Buenos dias," he greeted us sourly. "You have pesos 200?"

"Right here," Doug replied and counted the money out.

Several molting red hens strutted about at our feet, clearly starving. I had seen no signs of grass anywhere on the brown, parched earth. They picked at cracks in the deeply rutted cement floor, which was speckled with mounds of brown and white fowl poo. Some had also stuck to the side of my sandal.

"Two more honcho's? Your amigos? They come now?" The chief's gruff voice interrupted my contemplation of fowl excrement. He looked pointedly at Doug whose only response was a frown.

"Senor, Senorita. Americanos. They come now, please." The man scratched the black whiskers on his chin.

"He must mean Brooke and David," I said, turning to Doug who was mopping the sweat from his brow with a crumpled white handkerchief. "He's waiting for them to arrive."

"Si, si." The man looked at me and nodded. "Witness! Comprehende? Must be dos witness." And he held up two fingers.

I whispered to Doug, "What do we do now? Damn Brooke and David for leaving. Apparently we need two witnesses."

Doug hesitated for a moment then smiled at the Chief.

"No problemo," he shouted. "Two friends wait outside. Two witness. I get."

I wondered why he was speaking that way. "Come on," he said, grabbing my hand and dragging me outside. The battered old cab was parked where we had left it, the sun glaring blindingly off its metal roof. Fortunately, the driver had understood we wanted him to wait. He was squatting on the sidewalk, sucking the last of the nicotine from a hand-rolled cigarette.

"You come with me inside," Doug said, dragging him to his feet. The man looked alarmed and drew back. Doug reached into his wallet and pulled out some pesos.

"Here. Please come." He pointed at me. "Senorita, me, we get marry." He yanked the wedding ring from his pocket and flashed it at the man. "You comprehende? Come, be our amigo."

The cabbie eyed the pesos and suddenly was enlightened. Breaking into a wide grin, he grabbed the money. By now a few pedestrians had gathered, their sombreros bobbing on their heads as they shuffled nearer to see what these crazy gringos were doing. I noticed an older man with a missing eye paying close attention. I whispered to Doug and he turned to him.

Pulling more money from his pocket, he beckoned the one-eyed man forward and tried to explain. Our cabbie maybe understood for he joined the entreaties. The two Mexicans exchanged a few excited words then number two nodded, reached for the pesos and he, too, grinned, showing a full set of yellow teeth. I linked my arms with the two Mexicans and dragged them inside where the chief waited. He had lit up a fat cigar in our absence and was puffing feverishly. I wasn't sure if smoke was getting into his eye or if he was winking at me.

"What amigos these?" he asked suspiciously. "This no good. Must be hombres you know dos years." Again he held up two fingers and again he winked, belying the severity of his voice.

"Hai, Hai," I replied anxiously. "Wacalymasu! Sore wa watashi no tomadachis arimasu."

Doing my best to convince him, I clamped my arms around our two witnesses in a show of familiarity.

"You idiot! Why are you speaking Japanese?" Doug sounded puzzled.

"My mistake . . . I'm nervous, sorry."

Our two new friends were surprisingly savvy. They continued grinning and repeatedly shook hands with us, pumping vigorously with damp palms and bony fingers. One even tried to embrace me. The chief looked disgusted, removed the cigar from his mouth, spat, stubbed the cigar on the floor, put it in his breast pocket, held his hand up for silence and started the ceremony . . . . in Spanish, of course.

By now we had an audience as most of the townspeople seemed to have crowded into the open-air building. Runny-nosed children clung to their mother's skirts and older boys chased squealing girls across the room while the adults looked on shyly. Some groups hung back around the arches; the more outgoing ones edged forward curiously. A real party atmosphere was developing. I quietly kicked a red fowl away when it rubbed its molting body against my legs. A spotted dog with its ribs sticking out skittered across the floor and chased it. The fowl ran, squawking outside with the dog barking in hot pursuit. The chief droned on, still occasionally winking at me—or so I thought—for he no longer smoked, eliminating the possibility of smoke irritation. We understood not a word but whenever he left a pregnant pause, Doug nudged me and we chorused "Si, Si," bringing a look of satisfaction to the chief's face.

We were up to our third or fourth 'si' when there was a minor disturbance. Two young constabularias marched into the room dragging a manacled man between them. I assumed he was a prisoner, and possibly violent, for they didn't take the risk of walking around us but dragged him the shortest route possible, bursting right between us and the chief. I leaped back, avoiding the hapless prisoner's foul breath, but the chief never hesitated in his soliloquy. I looked in the direction of the disappearing prisoner as I heard the clanging, metal sound of what must have been a cell door out back.

My lack of attention annoyed the chief who stopped what he was saying, pinned me with a baleful glare, and hollered, "Si?"

"Gracious! Yes! Si, Si," I cried and Doug burst out laughing. The proceedings must have ended for our marriage celebrant spread some papers out on a nearby table and beckoned us to come over and sign. As I bent forward, some limp bougainvillea fell from my hair onto the certificate. Carried away by the moment, I snatched it up and tossed it to the crowd where it was caught by a nimble young girl. At the conclusion of the signing, the chief stamped the paper, gave us one copy then asked for an additional one hundred pesos which I assumed was the penalty for our witness exchange.

Most of the audience followed us outside and watched as we climbed back into our wedding cab. Someone had kindly sprinkled it with blossoms and attached a length of rope to the back piece of bumper that still remained. The significance of the rope was lost on me but I showed my appreciation by bowing to the crowd. Our cabbie and new best friend fastened his fly after peeing against a cactus. He then climbed behind the wheel and the taxi lurched out into the road, dislodging several blossoms and barely missing a pair of mating dogs. Doug and I laughed all the way back.

"Do you really think we are married?" I asked Doug.

"I think so. He stamped the paper. I'm amazed he could see it with that eye impediment. But let's make sure. We should stop off at the registry office in Seattle and do it again."

"It won't be quite the same," I said.

CHAPTER 41

The Honeymoon Ends Too Soon

The honeymoon was short-lived. On the plane back to Alaska, we discussed our future.

"I'm sorry we're starting our life together with money problems, honey." We had the privacy of an empty seat beside us. "Jean has wiped us out. She got the house and land, the Maui condo, The Eagle River property, and half of ATT. The Alaska Gulf was all I could save."

"Life is one big challenge," I replied, hiding my alarm. "Between us, we'll work it out."

Doug looked away. When he turned back, his eyes were clouded.

"I'm afraid there's more. I didn't want to tell you sooner and spoil our wedding . . . the friggin' off-shore oil wells at Prudhoe have come up dry."

"Oh my God," I gasped. "After all the money and work you have put into the Alaska Gulf. What are we going to do?"

"Yeah. All those delays have run conversion costs out of sight. But don't you worry your pretty head. I've got a plan."

"What? Sell the ship?"

"Not at all! Sell ATT and keep the Alaska Gulf. The trucking company would be a problem now with Jean as a vindictive half-owner. I've decided to turn the Alaska Gulf into a crab-fishing vessel. It won't take much work. I'll just have to add pumps to the below deck tanks. We have to keep the crab alive by continually pumping sea water through the tanks until we get back to the cannery."

"Is that all?" I was using my feet to push off my shoes as I spoke.

"Not quite that simple but it will be worth it. The king crab season last year turned into a real bonanza. The fleet caught thirty-three million pounds and several vessel owners became millionaires almost overnight."

"How long does the season last?"

"Until the Department of Fisheries calls it to a halt; it all depends on the amount of crab caught. They guard against over-fishing. Crew members work on a percentage of the catch and many of those returned home as rich young men last season."

"Well, babe, those prospects sound pretty good. What else needs to be done to be ready?"

"There are pot haulers, depth finders, loran, radar, hydraulic cranes and other incidentals to install. We'll need survival suits for the crew and life rafts. All damned expensive. We'll need about one hundred and fifty crab pots, enough to make a good haul but not enough for the weight to be a problem." He inhaled deeply. "It won't take long—once I have the money."

The airline hostesses had reached us with the lunch trolley. I could smell the reheated chicken in the air as Doug ordered two glasses of wine. For awhile, we ate in silence.

"I'm almost ready to sail now," Doug continued after emptying his plate. "Most of the Alaskan fishing fleet is in Seattle. I'll install the loran and radar in Hawaii and do the rest up there." He hesitated. "You aren't expecting a royalty check any time soon, are you?"

"Afraid not." I shifted uncomfortably in my seat. "And even if I was, it wouldn't be near enough. Won't selling your half of the truck company give you what you need?"

He beckoned the passing hostess to refill our glasses before continuing. As if seeking an answer in the wine, we both took a healthy swallow.

"Unfortunately, no. It costs a fortune to dock a ship that size and pay welders and electricians for such a long period. I still owe plenty."

"Try not to worry." I reached for his hand, hiding my rising alarm. This had to work. We needed to pay for a home study for Benny and fares from India for him and an escort. I had to arrange a Seattle rental and I desperately wanted to buy a home of our own. I looked absently at my bare feet and released Doug's hand. He should have told me this sooner. But what could I have done? I had thrown my lot in with his and it was too late to back out.

Back in Fairbanks, Doug had found a buyer for the truck company. The disappointing price was not enough to pay all the debts and outfit the ship. If he missed the season, we were bankrupt. I tried to quell rising fear.

Looking at Benny's photo for the thousandth time, I thought, this could not have been all for nothing! Suddenly I resented Doug for not being more forthright from the start. He was forever the eternal optimist.

Days later, I drove him once again to the Fairbanks airport. He planned to fuel the ship and sail from Hawaii to Seattle with a skeleton crew of three men. They would be ready to pull up anchor as soon as the ATT sale money was in the bank, thus enabling Doug to pay off the shipyard. I would remain behind, holding his power of attorney, until the sale was finalized.

"Just to fuel a vessel that size is costly. Running her twenty-four hours a day soon sucks it up," Doug said, glancing at me as I concentrated on the road." I've got to come up with money quick if we're to have her ready for the crabbing season."

"How long since you've sailed a ship?" I was a mix of emotions; anxious, annoyed, yet worried about him and the upcoming trip. "It's a long haul from Hawaii to Seattle."

"Years. But, like riding a bike, you never forget. Might just have to update my captain's license, that's all."

At the terminal, he removed his luggage from the back seat. I turned off the engine and climbed out.

"Give me a hug, pet . . . I'll be worried until you arrive safely in Seattle . . . I'll find us somewhere to live before then."

He held me a little longer, a little tighter than usual.

"Piece of cake, honey. I'll call you ship-to-shore every day."

I remained in the parking lot, watching the sky until his plane took off and disappeared from sight. Despite the worry, I was thrilled to be moving to Seattle. Doug loved Alaska but there was no way I wanted to spend another winter in that harsh climate.

CHAPTER 42

Goodbye Alaska

I lay in bed, looking at those hated wood-veneered walls and thinking about how my life was about to change yet again. The apartment was silent. I had already sold the birds and the waterfall. There was only some last-minute packing to do.

Life was passing too quickly. I was almost forty yet it didn't seem so long ago that I had left Vietnam. All those people that I had cared about, I never saw them again. All except Al Slugocki; a Special Forces sergeant major I knew in Vietnam. He and I still kept in touch. In fact, he had invited me and Doug to sail down the Amazon River with him as soon as we could arrange it. Since retiring from the military, he ran a paddle wheeler up and down the Amazon, taking wealthy patrons on charter fishing tours.

It was hard to believe that I had once been in fear for my life. I remembered one incident and chuckled. While I was still living on the houseboat, I had received a frantic phone call from my sister, Clarice, a very level-headed nurse, living in Australia.

"June, is your phone tapped?" she whispered, her voice disjointed with fear.

"No, Claire, of course not. Why do you ask?"

243

"Mum asked me to phone you and warn you." She sounded breathless. "She wouldn't dare call you herself. In fact, she drove into town to use a public phone to call me and ask that I contact you."

"What's all this cloak and dagger stuff? Have you all lost your senses?"

"No. Mum thought her phone might be tapped. Two Tamworth police constables drove out to the dairy to see her today. She was nervous as hell when she saw the police car, immediately thinking you were in trouble."

I could imagine the arrival of a police car stirring my very conservative, ultra law-abiding mother.

"What did they want?"

"The FBI called them from the States, looking for you. They had apparently been keeping tabs on you and your boat disappeared. They wanted to know where you had gone."

I imagined the scene. Nothing ever happened in Tamworth, except a very occasional robbery or cows loose on the road. The local constabulary must have almost dropped the phone when they heard the FBI on the line. The visit to my mother would have been top priority.

"Relax," I said. "They were most likely keeping tabs on me for my own protection. I've done nothing wrong." Laughing, I had hung up. I smiled at the memory, visualizing the stir it would have caused in that country town.

I stretched and climbed out of bed. I didn't have to go to the truck yard; the new owners had already taken over and I was merely tidying up final details. Besides the actual business sale, there were permits and other relevant items to be transferred. It was a bit complicated, involving tax credits and other stuff I didn't fully understand.

I made coffee and put some bread in the toaster. While waiting, I gazed at my suitcases standing in the living room corner where the aviary once stood. The room looked bare . . . it had lost its heart already.

One suitcase was full of varied fur coats which I had acquired while living in Alaska. I worried about wearing them in the lower forty-eight. The newspapers had recently been full of stories about anti-fur demonstrations. Crowds had gathered outside both Frederick & Nelson's and Nordstrom's in Seattle, and the protesters eventually forced the closing of the fur departments. The same thing was happening all over the country. Women who were insensitive enough to wear fur were chased down streets and pelted with eggs. That never occurred in Alaska, of course, where many of us wore fur. I pondered the egg-pelters, certain they wore leather shoes and ate meat. The world has always been full of hypocrisy!

After pouring my coffee, I sat at the breakfast bar. My eyes wandered by habit to Benny's framed photo. "Not much longer, baby," I said, peering into his dark, velvety eyes. Now that Doug and I were married and everything was ready in India, we just needed that home study. In Seattle, that would be first priority. I had already phoned a Washington adoption agency and set up an appointment.

It was hard to believe that almost five long years had passed in Alaska. I admired the spirit of the people (not the Johnny-come-lately, lower forty-eight workers who were there only for money). Alaskans reminded me of Aussies. They were down-to-earth and open to challenge. They were survivors! The country had its beauty: clear skies and craggy, pristine mountains; spectacular waving lights of the Borealis on a cold, clear night.

It had been a unique and wonderful experience but I was more than ready for some year-round sunshine.

Little did I know that I was exchanging snow and ice for rain. Seattle is infamous for its long, gray, wet winters and is aptly known as 'The Evergreen State'. One comic summed it up by saying, "You never grow old in Seattle . . . you only rust away."

Al's vessel.

On the Amazon.

My dear friend Al, and Doug, on the banks of the Amazon.

CHAPTER 43

Hullo Puget Sound

A week later, I settled into our rental home on picturesque Vashon Island in the Puget Sound. Vashon is one of the many small islands that surround Seattle. This one had no connecting bridge so it was sparsely populated. The Seattle ferry service ran regularly, transporting workers to and from downtown. Most passengers drove their cars onto the massive lower deck and came upstairs to grab a coffee and read the newspaper during the short journey.

Our rental home was located in a minimally-populated, bush-land area which I knew Doug would enjoy as much as I did. After Alaska, so much lush green and blue scenery felt like heaven. It was not uncommon to see soft-eyed deer grazing in our large, unfenced yard and nearby fields were scattered with sheep and long-haired, Scottish cattle.

The two-story timber house contained spacious, open rooms, new enough that the delicious smell of cedar still clung to their walls. I bought a series of braided rag rugs and tossed them onto the hardwood floors. By the time Doug was due, I had installed a rabbit in a large cage—outside this time—and a miniature goat called Baby Baa. I bought bicycles for me and Doug and a smaller one with training wheels for Benny. Baby Baa accompanied me on my afternoon rides, running beside the rear wheel much to the amusement of drivers in the occasional passing cars.

Comfortable, second-hand furniture was acquired from a family who were leaving for California and the place was soon looking homey enough to pass a home study.

I had spent a few nervous days when Doug had been unable to reach me on the ship-to-shore radio but, otherwise, his trip was uneventful. He arrived safely, proclaiming the vessel performed beautifully, exceeding his expectations. The older vessel had a narrow beam which Doug always claimed was more seaworthy than the newer, broader ones.

My daily routine was leisurely to the point of dullness but I loved the change of pace and the peace of my surroundings. Not so for Doug who left early each day, heading to the Ballina docks where he worked frantically until returning home late at night. It was the closest we had come to living like a 'normal' couple and the first time I had been a proper housewife since being married to the sheep farmer in my teenage years so long ago.

I thought of those years. It was another life and one that was hard to believe had actually happened. I was a different person then . . . innocent and ignorant. I thought of my babies and the grief I had suffered. How their deaths had altered my life . . . altered me. Had they not died, I would never have left my husband. To this day, I would have been a farmer's wife— untravelled, unsophisticated, uncomplicated—but wrinkled prematurely from the hot Australian sun. It was strange to imagine and I suddenly felt a little sad for the family that would have been. I thought of my baby, the only child who had lived at all. That tiny little thing, lost somewhere in a Tamworth cemetery. The next time I went to Australia, I should try to have a headstone placed on her small grave.

And then I thought of Benny! If all those other things hadn't happened, he would not be finding a home, a future.

Three children I lost . . . I had always wanted a large family. So many homeless children I had seen . . . far too many. But at last, after so many years, my dream was about to bear fruit. I couldn't have done it without Doug. My heart warmed with love. He was doing this for me. Of that I was sure. How lucky I was to have found such a good man.

The Vashon house and my car.

CHAPTER 44

Adoption Started

Merrily Rippley, a pleasant woman in her late thirties, could have been the spokesperson for any PTA group. She was the director of WACAP, a private adoption agency in Port Angeles, Washington. She and her husband had adopted several children and the WACAP offices were located on their neatly manicured farm. I sat nervously in her office, looking out the window at some grazing horses, as she rifled through my papers from India. Doug sat beside me holding my hand. This public display was unusual for him.

"Well, it is highly irregular that you have located the child and passed him through the Indian courts yourself," she stated in a solemn voice. "I don't know how you did it but we will need to check it out to make sure the child is actually an orphan. As you must be aware, some desperate overseas parents sell their children."

"I would never take a child from its parents." I bristled. "Our helper overseas is an American nun and I can assure you she would not be involved in anything underhanded. Our only motive is to help a child, not harm one."

"I'm glad to hear you say that." Merrily relaxed a little. "WACAP's motto is 'We find parents for children, not children for parents'. There is a big difference. So, if we are to get started, you need to write a check to WACAP for two thousand dollars before you leave. That will cover the costs of checking out your Indian court papers and doing the home study. Should you fail that, there is no refund. Fares and other costs can come later."

"No problem," Doug spoke up.

"But it is a problem that you have not met the minimum-time requirement to show marriage stability." She picked up the marriage certificates, both of them, which sat on the desk in front of her.

"Can't you relax the rules a little?" Doug asked. "By the time you have completed the home study—you did say it would take two or three months—we will have been married long enough. This poor boy has waited too long already."

Merrily frowned. "You have to understand the agency's position. We are one of the biggest on the West Coast and we can't chance an adoption disrupting through divorce or any other breakdown. We would soon be out of business and a lot of children would suffer."

"Ours won't disrupt." My positive words belied my fear. Her words about home-study failure had sent a tremor through my heart. "I've waited years for this. I am totally committed to Doug and our child."

"I'll do my best." She rose. "I'll start this week by sending Lisa out to visit you in your home. As your caseworker, she will visit you periodically and you will need to furnish her with contact numbers for neighbors and others who have known you and can vouch for you. Being new in the area is another problem but we will contact those who knew you in Alaska."

I glanced out the window again and my hands shook slightly. No one in Alaska knew me well enough to recommend me for motherhood. I desperately hoped they would at least focus on my good character.

A school bus pulled in at the end of the driveway. I saw a group of children hop off and run towards the house; they were brown, yellow, and white. As Doug stood to take our leave, I crossed my fingers.

From that day onwards, I kept my house in spotless condition. I had never previously baked bread and seldom made cakes or cookies but I bought a pile of cookbooks and started giving Julia Child a run for her money. Our home was continually warm from the oven and filled with the tantalizing aromas of baking goodies. Soon, Doug and I began putting on weight. If Lisa dropped in unexpectedly, she would find the perfect wife and future mother.

She did drop in on us unexpectedly one day . . . just as I discovered Baby Baa had escaped his leash and eaten my newly-planted flower bed.

"You rotten sod," I shouted, chasing him with a stick. "You stay away from my flowers, you four-legged bastard!"

"Oh my! Caught you at a bad time, did I?" Lisa cooed.

I wiped the sweat from my face and smiled stiffly, trying to recover.

"Sorry, Lisa. I don't usually swear," I lied. "It's a bad habit from hanging around truckies too long." I thought it best not to mention my Vietnam days. "Come inside while I put the coffee on. I've just made a delicious chocolate cake."

When she left an hour later, I knew I had talked too much. Nerves had made me garrulous and I made a mental note to be more careful in the future; it would be disastrous if we failed the home study. I was washing the cups and saucers when Doug phoned from the Ballina shipyards.

"Lisa just left, Doug." I didn't give him a chance to speak. "She heard me swearing at the damned goat. Do you think it will hurt us?"

"I doubt it, babe. Depends on what you were saying."

"Nothing too bad . . . but what do you want?"

"We need to have a serious talk, pet. Our money situation is critical. There's plenty more we have to purchase and back debts are piling up. If I don't get money somewhere, and quick, we won't be going fishing next month. Take the ferry and meet me at Starbucks on First Avenue. I've got a plan involving you."

A few days later, Doug and I were again on a plane. This time, we were heading to San Francisco on United Airlines.

"It's a good thing you learned about these government loans," I said.

Doug looked up from the sport's page he'd been reading.

"Yeah. I'm grateful to that Hispanic fisherman who told me about it. The government is trying to encourage female and minority involvement in agricultural and fishing endeavors. That's why I can't apply for the loan myself and that's why I had to turn ownership of the Alaska Gulf over to you."

"It's a big gamble, Doug. I'm not a citizen, only a legal resident. They might turn me down."

"Stop worrying, honey. I told them all that. They wouldn't waste their time calling us down for this interview if that was a problem."

I twisted a strand of hair around my finger, still not convinced.

"And why do we have to borrow so much? One-point-one million seems a huge amount."

"We'll make that back in three good years. Don't be such a worrywart. The problem is, buying the vessel, then overhauling the engine and converting her, has cost almost three million. I used the Cook Inlet property as collateral. Now that Jean owns the property I have to refinance."

He turned back to his newspaper, ending the conversation. I sat there, my elbow resting on the drop-down table, my head in my hand. All my life I had paid cash for everything. I had never owned a credit card. It was hard to comprehend that I was now the owner of a big old ship and about to go into debt for more than a million dollars. I closed my eyes and said a little prayer, a habit I seemed to be falling into of late.

CHAPTER 45

Preparing For King Crab Season

After we received the money, Doug spent long hours at the Ballina boatyards, racing to get all the new fishing gear installed in time for the start of the season. The Alaska Gulf was just one of the large fleets preparing to head north to Dutch Harbor for the king crabbing.

I stayed home every day, enjoying the unfamiliar luxury of time. Now I was becoming just like my mother and my sisters, doing everyday things like cooking, cleaning, gardening, (a new experience), and playing with my pets.

Doug returned late each night and I caught up on my reading while waiting, trying not to think about the large amount of money I owed the government.

Doug kept reassuring me, tossing out figures in the millions, claiming that's how much the crabbers had made the previous year, 1980. He called me a pessimist. I retaliated by calling him an optimist and claimed I was a realist. Still, right or wrong, he was the captain. I found a T-shirt in a Seattle store that had the words 'Right or Wrong, I am the Captain' printed on it. I bought it for him but he failed to see the humor and wouldn't wear it.

It was late afternoon on a beautiful autumn day. I rode my bike down to the dock with Baby Baa running at my heels. No ferries were due in and it was all quiet. I climbed off the bike and sat in the grass on a slope overlooking the sound. The water was calm. In the distance, I saw the familiar green and yellow ferries chugging past. Behind them was the downtown skyline, a mix of old and modern buildings. The city planners had done well; Seattle was a pretty city. Rain or not, I was happy to live in such a locale.

I wondered if Benny would like it and tried to visualize what everything would look like through his eyes. I wondered would my blonde hair scare him. Briefly, I considered dying it dark to look more like the women he was accustomed to. At least, I will wear a long dress for our first meeting, I thought. Every time I thought about him, I became suffused with happiness.

The sun was dropping low, reflecting in pink tinges off the snowy peak of Mount Rainier. Such a spectacular backdrop to the city, I sighed with pleasure. There could be no greater place to raise children. Washington, with its Douglas fir forests and numerous lakes, was beautiful. Its cities were culturally diverse. We would never live in Australia as long as Benny was a child. It was still imprisoned within the hangover of that 'White Australia' policy and my son might be stared at down there. In Seattle, we would blend in perfectly.

All we needed now was more money and life would be perfect. I thought again of the huge amount I owed and shuddered. We had only six months to pay back the first quarter of a million. That crab season had better be a bonanza! I rose and picked up my bike. Baby Baa looked up before tugging out a last tuft of grass.

I entered the house, salivating at the smell of baking lamb in the oven. I was so pleased Doug liked it; many Americans did not. Consequently, the supermarkets never carried lamb but I found a butcher shop in Pike's Market that sold it—sometimes fresh from Wenatchee, other times, imported frozen from New Zealand.

I had finished setting the table when I heard Doug drive up. I met him at the door. He was carrying a potted geranium.

Here's a little housewarming gift, sweetheart," he said, thrusting it at me.

I took it to the kitchen sink and ran water over the dry soil while noting the red sale-price sticker on the side of the pot. As the water ran, Doug came up behind me and nuzzled my neck.

"I'm a lucky man," he mumbled through my hair.

I turned and threw my arms around his neck.

"Let me take a shower, honey," he said. "I'm all sweaty from a long day . . . Dinner smells good."

"Okay, babe," I replied. "I'll pour us a glass of wine." I was opening a bottle from the recently discovered St. Michelle's Winery when Doug re-entered the room.

"We'll be ready to sail next week," he said, "I've signed on eight crew members. They seem like a pretty good bunch and all but one are experienced."

I nodded and sipped my merlot.

"The day before we sail I need you to come down and buy the ship's supplies."

"Why, Doug? I've never shopped for an army of men in my life and I would have no idea what quantities to buy."

"Live and learn, honey. Live and learn. We have special places for buying in bulk and they'll help with calculations. We'll need enough for several weeks. Besides the crew, there is Finn—the engineer—and you and I. A total of eleven."

I choked on my wine. "Me?" my voice went shrill.

"Of course, you! You didn't think I'd go to sea without you, did you?"

"Yes I did! What about our home study?"

"They must have visited us enough by now."

"And what about Benny's arrival?" I was aghast.

"You'll be back well before then. We must have a cook, honey. I'm relying on you."

I crossed to the table and blew out the lit candles while trying not to lose my temper. I knew Doug loved me very much but he was not a romantic person. I was surprised when he brought home a plant for me—even a half-priced, dying one. Was he trying to butter me up or was the gesture genuine?

"And what if we're not finished in time? I would hate you forever."

"Then I'll drop you ashore and the men and I will have to fend for ourselves. Sweetheart, you sound as if you love this boy you've never met more than you love me."

"What a terrible thing to say, Doug. I do everything to help you. I've never said no when many women would. Just this once, I really don't want to go." I felt shocked by Doug's expectation.

"I know you help me, honey. And, if you come this one time, I promise I will get you back on time and I will never ask you to go again." He stepped over to where I was standing and tried to kiss me. I twisted my head, feeling as if I was being blackmailed.

CHAPTER 46

Heading North

I stood in the pilothouse as the drug guys came aboard with their dogs. The trained canines sniffed their way through the crew's dorm on the lower deck, finding nothing. If they had, the culprit would have been thrown ashore immediately. Prior to sailing, each crew member had been required to take a drug test and produce their clean 'bill of health'.

The Alaska Gulf was a 'dry' ship and Doug had personally searched the crew's area for booze. Even the captain and the cook had to forgo wine while at sea; alcohol and crab fishing did not mix.

The crew couldn't even get life insurance. Crabbing Alaskan waters was, and still is, said to be the most dangerous job in America. The Bering Sea is reputed to suffer the most violent storms on the planet. The Bureau of Labor Statistics listed that area as having taken over 2070 lives since recordkeeping had started.

I looked out the wide expanse of pilothouse windows. Ours was located at the stern of the vessel. In front of me, the deck was stacked high with one hundred sixty empty crab pots. The metal cages measured five-foot square and were covered with strong webbing. When full, each one could hold over a hundred monster king crabs. I call them 'monster' because they dwarf all other species of crab. The largest have been measured with a leg span of six feet; however, I had learned that the average one had a span of a yard and weighed 10-12 pounds.

Those crab pots were so heavy that I wondered how the men could handle them—even with the help of machinery—when we began rolling in heavy seas. Doug said the stacks had been known to shift and overturn ships in raging weather if they weren't tied down properly.

A powerful A-frame of solid black metal held an array of huge sodium lights which were directed at the deck and surrounding water. They would be needed when we had to haul pots twenty-four hours a day.

I had recovered from my resentment and now looked forward to this new experience, trusting Doug's assurances that I would be back in time. The men seemed like a decent group, if a bit rough; all young with strong backs. Except our engineer! He appeared to be about forty and looked like life had dealt him a bad hand. He needed a good shave, his fingernails were black and he smelled strongly of stale tobacco. No one knew his real name . . . everyone called him Finn, a reference to his nationality.

I ran my hands over the smooth timber of the steering wheel. Doug had told me it was now ornamental only. When the vessel wasn't on autopilot, Doug steered it by a small, silver handle. I found it hard to believe that so small a lever could guide such a big piece of machinery.

The floor vibrated beneath my feet and I was aware of the continual throb of the engine. I found the sound rather comforting. Doug said 'the old girl' took quite awhile to warm up. She had already been running for a couple of hours. After she was switched on, I had noticed the excitement begin to build among the crew.

It had taken the better part of yesterday to fill her with fuel which Doug said cost over fifty-thousand dollars and might not even last until the season's end. We could top her up, he said, when delivering our catch to the cannery in Dutch Harbor. I had followed him three decks below to view the engine room and was amazed at the size of the steaming hot, black and noisy space that held the gigantic machinery. Finn, shirtless and streaming sweat, wore earmuffs to mute the sound. I couldn't wait to get out of there and vowed never to return.

The air in the pilothouse still held a whiff of engine fuel but I didn't find it unpleasant. Restless, I wandered from portside to starboard, estimating it to be about twenty-five feet across, almost as wide as the ship's beam. Pausing in front of the built-in map table, I fingered the array of maps laid out beneath a lamp screwed into the timber. The table had a lip running around the edges to prevent things from slipping off. I moved to the captain's chair and climbed up into it. In two more hours we would be pulling out. I couldn't believe I was on my way back to Alaska so soon. Doug bustled in.

"Is the galley all squared away, honey?" he asked.

"Finished it yesterday. The cooler room is chock-a-block," I said, spinning in the chair to face him. "Two crew members helped me. I can't remember their names yet. The boxes were too heavy for me to lift."

"You didn't put anything in the bait fridges did you?"

"Of course not."

"And you did fasten the latches on the galley refrigerator, I hope."

"Relax, Doug. I'm a quick learner, you know."

"Sorry, honey. I just have to double-check everything. It's too late once we're underway."

I slipped off the high chair. "If there's nothing for me to do right now, I'm going to practice my flute for awhile and keep out of everyone's way. You're all so busy with last minute things."

"You do that, honey. I'm glad you took those lessons in Seattle."

By early afternoon, we pulled away from the dock and it was more exciting than I expected. I stood at Doug's elbow, looking out the long window at our crew who were all standing on deck. There was a tangible anticipation amongst them. What would the next few weeks bring? What dangers would they face? Would they escape injury? Would they come home with pockets full of money? Fishermen were gamblers. There were no guarantees. If the ship made money, they made money, receiving a percentage of the catch. Men were known to go ashore with tens of thousands of dollars in their pockets after only a few short weeks.

As we slowly passed the few remaining fishing boats still at the docks, some tooted their horns in acknowledgement of our departure. Our boys shouted and gestured to deckhands they knew on other vessels.

On the trip north, there wouldn't be much for the crew to do until we reached the fishing grounds days later. However, it was a busy time for Doug and Finn.

Being a Saturday, the Puget Sound was filled with hundreds of small leisure craft. They darted this way and that. Many small boats, apparently oblivious to the marine rules, crisscrossed in front of us.

Our ship's horn shattered the air, making me jump.

"Look at that sonofabitch!" Doug exploded. "Did you see how close he cut across in front of me? Doesn't he know I have the right of way? It takes a vessel this size forever to slow down and I could have cut the asshole in two. It would have served him right!"

I looked at the anger lines on his face and decided to change the subject.

"Are we going to travel up through Canada's inland passage?" I asked hopefully.

"No. We're a day late so I'll cut across the open sea. It's rougher but faster and it'll help the new kid get his sea legs before we start fishing."

The M/V Alaska Gulf.

In calm waters. Doug and a crew member.

Pilot House.

CHAPTER 47

The Bering Sea

I woke sensing that something was wrong, and sat up in the bunk.

Doug spent around eighteen to twenty hours a day running the ship. Occasionally, Finn came up and took the controls, giving Doug a break; no one else was qualified to do it.

Doug was sleeping soundly beside me but space was so tight with both of us squeezed into the bunk that we rarely slept at the same time. I hadn't heard him climb in and my sense of unease persisted.

Finn always smoked when he was on the bridge; as he was now, I could smell the smoke. I listened intently. The engines throbbed smoothly, reassuring as ever. I heard no voices, so assumed that Finn was up there alone. Smelling the cigarette smoke once more, I jerked my head towards the few short steps separating the cabin from the bridge. That was it! The tobacco smell was different . . . it was not Finn's brand of cigarettes.

I climbed to the floor then negotiated the few stairs leading up to the pilothouse.

"Where's Finn?" I asked Bo, the young man at the controls.

"He was tired so I took over for him."

"Do you know what you're doing?"

"Sure, it's not that hard," Bo replied.

"Then maybe I should have a go."

He shot me a scornful look as I disappeared back down the steps.

Doug was breathing heavily. I was sure he must be exhausted but he seldom showed it. Loath to wake him, I stood there uncertainly for a few moments wondering what to do. Finally, I decided I had to let him know.

"Doug, honey, wake up." I shook him gently. No response. I shook him harder, all the while hating what I was doing. Finally, he stirred.

"Wha . . . what?" he spoke groggily.

"I think you need to check on the bridge. Finn isn't up there and one of the crew is running her."

"How do you know?" he was still half asleep.

"I smelled cigarette smoke and I knew it wasn't Finn's so I checked."

Groaning only slightly, he clambered from the bunk and climbed the steps with me in tow.

"Where's Finn?" he asked the man at the controls who repeated what he had said to me. Fully awake now, Doug checked the controls.

"Good God Almighty!" he spluttered after a few minutes. "We're way off course. Another twenty minutes and we would have run aground." He quickly made some adjustments and, soon after that, I felt the ship begin to curve. The young man apologized, embarrassed.

"It's not your fault," Doug conceded. "It's Finn's. You never desert your watch. That sonnofabitch is going to get a piece of my mind. Thank God my wife has the nose of a bloodhound."

We had reached the infamously dangerous Bering Sea and, after much debate about location, dropped our first pots. I watched curiously as crew members crawled inside the pots and baited each one with clumps of smelly herring. Once baited, the cumbersome cages, weighing six hundred pounds each, were dropped overboard in lines of twenty. They were attached to each other by what was called a 'string'. Additionally, each pot had a brightly colored orange buoy attached to it by a long rope. The buoys floated on the surface, signifying the position of each pot on the dark, icy cold ocean floor some 600 feet below. King crab lives only at depths of 400 feet or more. After one string was set, we then moved some distance further away to drop the next string, hedging our bets. Even with modern technology, it was a bit of a gamble trying to guess at what spots the crab might be in abundance. We repeated this process, moving overnight to another position, until all one hundred and sixty pots had been dropped and their latitude and longitude registered. Doug said we had to let the pots 'soak' for at least twenty-four hours before the men hooked onto the lines and hauled them up; a task requiring experienced men.

Meanwhile, I was learning what it was like to cook for a tribe of hungry, young, sea-soaked men. They all said my cooking was as good as their mothers. It probably was but I knew they wanted to stay on the good side of the cook. However, after a few days, they almost mutinied over my coffee. I agreed to discontinue making the morning brew and they added that chore to their duties.

Once the work started, they slept little and ate a lot—usually five times a day. T-bone steaks and veggies were the most popular and I kept a cauldron of hearty soup simmering at all times. They could always help themselves to a bowl if they had a free moment.

When the vessel was rolling, I learned to keep upright by standing before the big steel stove with my feet apart, firmly braced. The saucepans were screwed into metal holding-bars and I placed small quantities into enormous pots to allow for splashing (this was before the wonderful invention of those swinging stoves).

Ice cream was the big problem. The crew usually helped themselves to it at night while I was sleeping and they seldom remembered to latch the refrigerator door. I came in one morning after the weather had turned rough. The refrigerator door was swinging and the contents were in a pile at my feet. I cussed each crew member individually as I crawled about on the violently heaving floor, picking up broken jam jars, egg yolks and busted shells, mashed apple pie, and legs of ham doused in yellow custard. Streams of milk ran first this way and then that, flowing with the movement of the ship, splashing through the mess and soaking my pants as I crawled about, dodging broken glass.

The first week passed quickly. The catch wasn't great so we moved to a new area. In between cooking, if the sea was calm I sat on the small upper deck, inhaling the brisk air and practicing my flute. I had learned to play 'Bring on the Clowns' reasonably well and I related to the title.

Even when the sun occasionally cut through the heavy, low clouds, the weather was endlessly freezing. Always wearing woolen headgear and a thick, ugly parka, I scanned the ocean often, searching for the telltale spout of a whale. They never came close to us but the dolphins were another matter. They came really close and crisscrossed playfully in front of the bow. I particularly liked watching them at night when they streaked sideways under the water, their tummies glowing phosphorous green in the lights.

The dark, icy sea mesmerized me but in a frightening way and with good reason. Five minutes in those deadly waters without a survival suit and I would be dead. I spent hours looking at its changing characteristics; deep, dark and foreboding one minute, light and frothy the next . . . and always interminable, far from any sight of land.

Emptying a pot.

Hauling a pot—not a good haul. No one's smiling.

CHAPTER 48

I was in a deep sleep when a solid force of ice-cold water sloshed into my face. Instantly I shot up, filled with dread. The single porthole of the cabin was hanging open and sea water was gushing in. The Alaska Gulf was rolling violently and the tall, narrow wardrobe at the foot of the bunk had broken from its moorings, leaning drunkenly over the bed.

Springing to the head of the bunk, I tried to slam the porthole shut and push the thick bolt into place. Between the force of the water and the stiffness of the hinge, I couldn't move it. Every time the ship rolled to port side, another flood of water gushed in. Were we sinking? What had happened? The cabin was high above the normal waterline. How could waves have reached this height?

Terrified, I hurried up to the bridge, struggling to hang onto the steel bars along the walls and not lose my footing. The wind outside was screaming so insanely loud that I couldn't even hear the engines. Dragging myself into the pilothouse, I was aghast to see every inch of our wide windscreens streaming under heavy water as if we were passing beneath a waterfall. In the seconds between the deluges, I caught glimpses of the monstrous waves rolling towards us. They moved in endless, fearsome rows all the way back to the misty horizon. I had heard stories about rogue waves and I strained to see if any single wall of water towered above the others.

Three of our crew members were crowded around Doug, looking really scared. Not so Doug. He was on the intercom, talking loudly to Finn in the engine room, but he appeared calm and in control.

"What's happened!?" I asked the crew members.

"One helluva storm has blown in from the north, that's what," one said.

"And our engine has picked a fuckin' great time to quit," the greenhorn said, his face drained of blood. "We're getting battered in the trough. If the engine doesn't start up soon, a broadside will capsize us."

Doug stopped calling to Finn and turned his attention briefly to me. "Don't panic," he said. "Finn will get the engines started. At least we're not top-heavy with pots. Thank God, we've already dropped them."

At that moment, another crew member wearing his bright orange survival suit dragged himself into the pilothouse. My eyes flew open wide.

"Waters coming over the port side and flowing through the crew's quarters, Doug," he gasped.

"What?" the other crewmen yelled in chorus.

"I'm gonna get into my survival suit!" one cried, heading for the steps.

One by one, the others slowly followed him, hanging tightly to the bars so as not to get thrown across the long pilothouse; men had been killed that way in seas like this.

"When you pass our cabin, please stop a minute and close the open porthole," I begged, trying unsuccessfully to keep the total panic out of my voice as I turned to Doug.

"I'm scared, Doug," I vastly understated my fear.

"Don't get your bowels in an uproar," he said. "Finn will get us started any minute. Once I can turn her nose into the waves, we'll be just fine. I've rode out worse than this."

His words did nothing to reassure me. About that time, I started silently praying. When the windscreen had a moment's respite from the blinding waterfall, I again saw waves resembling black, wet, heaving mountains. Shaking like a leaf in a blizzard, I fought to hold down bile. 'I'm in hell but it's not made of fire,' I thought.

My gaze kept returning to one section of the instrument panel. It resembled the face of a clock, with a white background and black numbers. Its center needle-like hand was also similar to that on a clock. At the furthest point, near the bottom on the right hand side of the dial, was a red-colored square. Doug had previously told me that the instrument measured the degree of the ship's list. The red patch was the danger zone. If the hand moved into that spot, it meant capsize. With every fresh broadside wave, the hand was reaching the red. Even in Vietnam during mortar attacks and when being shot at, I had never been this scared. I felt catatonic, unable to breathe.

When I could next see through the windows, I looked out onto the deck. The entire crew was there wearing their bright survival suits and hanging on tight so as not to be washed overboard. Waves continually crashed over us, sweeping away anything not nailed down and battering the men, who seemed to be staring fixedly at the furious sea, contemplating if and when they should release the life rafts and abandon ship. Suddenly it hit me. Doug and I were the only ones not wearing a survival suit. And, if we capsized, Finn could not escape from the engine room. The three of us had no chance.

"Where are our survival suits?" I yelled at Doug. He ignored me. Right then, the ship rolled so hard that it dropped away from under my feet; only space was beneath me. If I hadn't been hanging on tight, I would have tumbled across the pilothouse like a broken doll.

"Where the hell are our suits?" I rasped again after my feet crashed back to the floor with a thump, almost knocking the wind out of me. "I've gotta put mine on."

"Don't be stupid," he said. "Ignore the crew. You, Finn and I are safer here. We won't capsize. Those assholes are more likely to drown if they jump overboard."

"Don't lie to me!!" I screamed. "I have eyes. I can see the needle going into the red. How could you do this to us? Why didn't you get us survival suits? Doesn't the law require a survival suit for every member?" My chest was so tight I thought I might have a heart attack.

"Short of money and they won't save you anyway."

"Stop lying, Doug. If we survive this, I'll nev . . ." the words died on my lips. Through the sound of the howling wind and thrashing rain, I thought I heard another sound; through the deck jerking beneath my feet, I thought I felt a rapid shudder. Was I imagining it? Willing it? NO! Hallelujah! Hallelujah! The engine was running.

Ignoring me, Doug focused hard on the vessel—his pride and joy—and inch by precious inch in an ordeal of slow motion, he began to turn the pointed bow into the waves.

CHAPTER 49

Wasted Effort— Shattered Dreams

I would like to say that there was only that one bad incident during our king crab season but, unfortunately—although that first storm was the worst—as any crabber can tell you, life is a series of big and small disasters.

There was the time Finn got blind drunk on the whiskey he had smuggled into the engine room. Doug's best efforts failed to uncover it in that labyrinth of pipes, hoses and pulsating engines. Finn remained totally useless for two whole days while Doug struggled on, running between the engine room and the pilothouse.

There were times when Doug was required to act as ship's doctor, such as when he put twelve stitches into one man's leg.

Also, a heavy snow storm caused a 'white-out' at sea. It felt so eerie to be on a ship in semi-darkness with heavy snow blotting out both sky and ocean. I thought we had left the planet. That was soon followed by the ship icing up.

The heavier ice on one side had us listing dangerously and the men's best efforts could not seem to remove the ice fast enough. As quick as they chipped, more ice formed. In desperation, we pumped out much of our precious fresh water to balance the lopsided ship.

As the men became tired from the long hours of cold, hard work and our catch was not living up to expectations, the men became irritable and arguments began breaking out.

Since Doug was a hard taskmaster, behind his back, I heard a couple of them refer to him as Captain Bligh. On one occasion, I thought we were going to have a mutiny on our hands.

I have never considered myself a wimp but one is certainly put to the test on that treacherous ocean. Just like in Vietnam, I could go from total boredom to heart-stopping horror in mere seconds.

Throughout my life, I have trusted fate but I was beginning to think less about fate and more about God. I certainly called out to Him often while battling that part of His creation. The Bering Sea is not something any intelligent person takes lightly and those fishermen undoubtedly earn every cent.

The season did not end well. After many prosperous seasons, the king crab suddenly seemed to disappear. From a total fleet catch of 33,000,000 pounds the previous year, that season it plummeted to 3,000,000 pounds. Some said it was due to over-fishing. Greed always accounts for much of what happens in the world. The year earlier—when word spread about the fishing bonanza—investors from the lower forty-eight quickly formed companies. They bought ships, hired captains and crews and sent them north post-haste at the same time that we joined in. Coincidentally, about then, the water temperature changed, heating up by four or five Fahrenheit degrees. King crab thrives in deep, dark, icy water; those degrees of difference were crucial. Whether due to water temperature, over-fishing, or a combination of both, the king crab numbers decreased and have never returned to what they were previously.

As for The Alaska Gulf, we lost it. The season was so bad that any ship that had money owing on it was repossessed. There was such a glut of them that they couldn't bring a decent price at auction. And I ended up owing the government one-point-one million dollars in 1981 money.

The current fishing fleet is made up of true Alaskans as seen on that great television show, The Deadliest Catch. Whenever I watch, it brings back memories. I cheer for the men still doing that dangerous work but I'm glad I'm not out there.

CHAPTER 50

Benny Arrives

After losing The Alaska Gulf, we continued renting that pleasant home on Vashon Island.

Doug immediately took a job as a captain on someone else's vessel. This was not a fishing vessel but a smaller one used by an oil company for servicing an offshore oil-rig. Although we weren't exactly penniless, there was no way I could pay back the one-million-dollar-plus loan. Strangely, I wasn't overly depressed about the change of fortunes. Both Doug and I were entrepreneurial souls and I was confident we would rise again.

Our son's arrival had been delayed month after month, sending me into a paroxysm of frustration. Doug had barely left for sea when I got the long-awaited call that Benny was finally arriving. I prepared for my trip to New York with such joy that I was almost incoherent. No major event in my life, no marriage, no birth of any child, ever meant more to me than Benny's arrival.

Doug and I had paid for two airline tickets. One for Benjamin and one for the Indian man who had helped us to adopt him from that end. The man told us he would be escorting

Benny into New York, not Seattle, because other orphans he was bringing in at the same time, were going to the east coast.

For months, I had visualized beautiful scenes, over and over again, of Ben running into my open arms, a big smile on his little face and tears of joy streaming down his cheeks. Alas, reality so often fails us.

I waited at Kennedy Airport alone, disappointed that Doug was unable to be with me. The plane landed and every nerve-end tingled with excitement. So many emotions ran riot, so many thoughts filled my head. What would I say? What would I do? What would he do? Would he be scared? Of course, he'd be scared! I was wearing a long dress, knowing Indian women wore them but I was worried about my whiteness and blonde hair.

From the moment the plane's tires hit the ground, I fought an enormous lump in my throat. Craning my neck—stretching, peering—I searched the arriving passengers while my heart beat a crazy tattoo. People flowed out endlessly, running forward to embrace waiting loved ones all around me. As the crowd became a trickle and there was no sign of any little Indian child, fear spread like molten lava and I began to panic. Had he missed the plane? Had the Indians changed their mind about sending him? I didn't know where to turn, what to do. Alarm bells grew louder when I saw two serious-faced immigration officials hurrying towards me.

"Are you waiting for a little Indian boy?" one asked.

"Yes, I am." The words spilled out in a rush.

"I'm afraid there's a problem." A problem? My brain screamed as my purse fell to the floor and a million disastrous possibilities tumbled through my head.

"Yes. He traveled all that distance alone and he is so hysterical that we can't fingerprint him or take his photo."

The larger of the two men pinned me with an accusing stare.

"He's uncontrollable. We have considered calling a doctor to give him a shot to calm him."

Those words cut to my soul, filling me with instant, unreasoning guilt.

"Alone?" I stammered. "There was supposed to be an escort. I don't understand."

"One of the airline hostesses said a man got on the plane with him but he jumped up and left just before the plane took off," the immigration officer replied. "Now, follow us. I'm afraid we have had to lock the boy in an office. He was so traumatized that he broke free and ran through the airport. We had a hard time catching him."

My heart was tearing apart. What had happened? Why would the man I had paid to escort Benny leave him to fly alone? It was unlikely the little boy would have seen a plane up close before. He may not even have understood what others were saying as India had so many different languages.

Had anyone explained to him where he was going or why? How absolutely horrifying for any little six-year-old! Shock turned to anger.

We reached the office and one of the officers knocked on the door. A thin woman dressed in uniform let us in and inclined her head to a corner. My heart leapt at the sight of the very small, thin black boy huddled on the floor, screaming his heart out. Surely this was not him? I was expecting a six-year-old; this child looked more like a three-year-old.

The clothes I had sent to India swam on him. A shoe, way too big, half-hung off one foot; his other foot was bare.

As I approached my child, doing my best to look non-threatening, he jumped up and ran to the opposite corner like a trapped animal. His eyes bulged and he screamed so loud that his little face looked like one big open mouth and I could see his pink tonsils. I backed off and sat down on the floor at his level.

It wasn't easy but, with patience, we managed to get my writhing, distraught child into a taxi. I directed the driver to a hotel where we would spend the night. I warned the cabbie to lock the doors, terrified by the thought that my son might leap out into the heavy New York traffic and be lost forever.

Clinging tightly to the screaming little bundle, I entered the hotel, causing a few heads to turn. It was impossible to hold him while signing in. A kindly gray-haired black man came to my assistance. He was wearing a red-braided uniform which identified him as a hotel employee.

While lifting Ben from me, he calmed him with soothing words. Maybe it was his gentle aura, maybe it was his familiar skin color, but somehow he accomplished what no one else had. I felt totally inadequate and I think I was in shock.

As we took the elevator to our room, Ben's screaming quieted and his frail body shook with quiet sobs.

I have never forgotten the tenderness of that stranger. Inside the hotel room, we discussed the situation and decided to try giving Ben a bath. To our surprise, it did the trick.

When the man lowered the boy's body into the warm water, Ben's little face took on a look of surprise. I guess it was his first time to feel water that had been heated. His eyes widened and he stopped crying. Soon he started kicking the water. Shortly after that, he even smiled, just a little.

Later that night—as I looked down at the beautiful face and thick, curly hair of my sleeping child—I wept, broken-hearted by the experience that one so young had endured. If only I had the power to wipe the events from this little boy's mind but I didn't.

Weeks later, I learned the full story. It seems our 'escort' was planning to make extra money by bringing a group of six children over (receiving the money for a plane ticket from each adoptive parent, I suppose) but there were delays with the visas of the other children. I had been harassing him about the continual delays with Ben so he took him alone to the airport. On the plane, he settled Ben in then told him he was leaving for a few minutes to buy some candy for the trip . . . he never returned.

Adoption has many pitfalls and so much can go wrong. Thankfully, after that shocking start, things improved.

Benjamin proved to be a beautiful and smart child although I worried that nightmare trip had added one more scar.

Benny, dressed for his first winter and already adjusting.

CHAPTER 51

Called To Action Again

Benny and I were getting to know each other. Every day we rode our bikes down to the harbor where we looked at the boats and played in the nearby park. Benny loved the swings and screamed with laughter when I pushed him high.

I was learning his likes and dislikes. He loved green grapes but hated eggs. The first words of English he spoke were all nouns, mostly the names of animals we passed in the fields. I was surprised at how quickly he was picking up the language. In excited bliss, I shared Benny's progress with Doug each night via the ship-to-shore radio and counted each day until Doug was back with us.

Doug continued his job as captain on the charter vessel for the oil company. Occasionally he was able to return home to spend short periods with us. Benny loved him and always cried when he left.

Safety regulations required a ship to be kept at the Alaskan offshore platform at all times. It was monotonous work circling the rig twenty-four hours a day in case of emergency. Doug and his three-man crew had nothing to do except plough continually through rough seas around that towering, well-lit city in the ocean.

I guess it was pretty boring. So much so that it sent their cook insane. For three days, he held them all at bay with a carving knife. He would neither feed them nor allow them into the galley. Doug called the Coast Guard and they came aboard, subdued the man and took him away in a straitjacket. The last I heard, he was placed in a mental institution on the outskirts of Tacoma, Washington.

So, again, I was called into action . . .

"Honey," Doug said over the ship-to-shore radio. "Just this one last time, please. I need you. We've not eaten a decent meal in days. You must come . . . Over."

"Benny needs me, Doug. You ask too much of me . . . . Over."

"It's only for a week until we can get another permanent cook in here . . . Over."

"You said the last time was the last time. I can't keep doing this. I have a child now . . . Over."

"Aw, come on, honey. My sister will take Benny for the week. I'd do anything for you. I love you! Don't you love me? . . . Over."

"Damn you, Doug. Haven't I already proved how much I love you? Well, this is definitely the last time . . . Over and Out."

Well, it was the last time and I could imagine why that chap went crazy. It was still winter and dark most of the time. We circled in dark, choppy waters, our axis always being those bright lights towering constantly above us.

The highlight of each day was the routine visit of the helicopter to the platform above. When the weather was too bad, the pilot couldn't make it and there was nothing to see at all through the rain and fog except the massive pylons and the misty platform lights.

And do you remember me mentioning earlier that I was afraid of heights? Well my arrival on that particular vessel was one I will never forget.

The oil platform was not near any city but out in the middle of nowhere. To reach it, I had to take a commercial flight to Anchorage, change to a small private plane that dropped me in a barren, snow-covered field God knows where. A man I didn't know waited for me and drove me in a four-wheel drive to a high cliff on the edge of the Arctic Ocean in no man's land. I couldn't see the sea because it was a bed of ice. I couldn't see any vessel either.

"Where is the ship?" I asked the man as we stood in the windswept field.

"There. Can't you see it?" he pointed to a small, mast top barely visible above the edge of the cliff. "It is low tide now and you know these humongous Alaskan tides."

He was walking towards the edge of the cliff as he spoke and I followed, crunching over the ice-hard ground. Upon reaching the drop-off, I squinted down and there she was, a good thirty feet below; well-hidden from the sight of anyone on land.

"Doug!" I screamed. "I'm here."

A crew member looked up and waved, then went to fetch Doug. The whole welcoming committee appeared on deck.

"How the hell do I get down there?" I wailed.

"No problem, honey," he yelled as the crew got busy around him. "We're sending up the crane."

"The what?"

"The crane. We'll hang a crab-hauling container on it."

"There's gotta be another way."

"Not unless you want to stay up there for hours until the next high tide. And we've gotta get back to the platform."

Even as he spoke, the men were winching up a huge, cubic-shaped crate. It swung from the end of the crane, held aloft by thick chains. I shivered as I watched it banging up against the face of the cliff.

"Steady now," the man escorting me said as the metal crate reached the top and he grabbed it with both hands. With some difficulty, he pulled it in close to the bank. I took a deep breath and started to climb in. The sides were about three and a half feet high. I strained to get one leg across before I gagged on the stink and noticed the pieces of putrid shellfish stuck along the edges. It was a tall stretch and, when I was halfway in and halfway out, the man operating the crane lifted it. In a panic, I yelled and fell over the edge, crashing onto the wet, slimy floor.

Shaken, I picked myself up, reached for the thick, rusted chain, and clung for dear life. It was a slow descent with my unwieldy transport repeatedly bashing into the cliff before twirling seawards. I landed on the deck with a bone-jarring crash, and only after hearing the men's applause, did I open my eyes.

"We're all starving!" Doug welcomed me and hustled me down to the galley.

"Cook us something quick." And, with that, he was gone.

Alone in the small galley, my blood ran cold. Have you ever heard the sound of a metal hull cutting its way through thick sea ice? And with the galley at sea-ice level, it sounded worse than a thousand chalks scraping over a blackboard. Gritting my teeth, I tried to ignore a splitting head-ache as I dragged stale food from the refrigerator.

CHAPTER 52

Learning About Benny

After a very long week, I was home again. Benny had learned enough English that it was time to start thinking of enrolling him in school. Still I delayed, wanting to keep him to myself a bit longer. Since moving to Vashon, I had started attending church; grateful, I suppose, for my survival and my blessings. Benny was enrolled in the local Sunday school.

Doug was home from the vessel for a short break. I left him to finish his dinner while I put Benny to bed.

After tucking Ben in, I sat beside him to read a bible story. He listened quietly for awhile before interrupting me.

"Mum, this man Jesus is nice but he never came to India." He said.

"Benny, I don't know what you mean, dear."

"Well the story says he loves little children. And the Sunday school teacher told us that he takes little children to live with him when they die."

"Then I'm sure she must be right." I answered, not sure of where this was heading.

"No she wasn't," he answered, "Babies died, lots of them, where I lived. We dug a big hole and threw dirt on them." He wrinkled his small face and added "Yuk . . . And Jesus never once came. So you see he doesn't go to India . . ."

I was overcome with sadness but I was discovering that many of Benny's recollections were poignant.

I had noticed a small scar on the top of his forehead. While washing his lovely thick hair, I discovered several more scars on his scalp.

"How did you get these marks, Benny?" I asked.

"I fell out of a coconut tree." He answered, not looking up from his coloring book.

"How high could you climb, dear?"

"All the way to the top. That's where the coconuts are and I was hungry." He stopped coloring and looked at me as if to say I should have known that.

"That's a long way to fall," I said, "You must have hurt yourself bad. Did you cry?"

"No," he replied matter-of-factly, "I cried once but nobody came so I never cried anymore."

How often I wanted to scoop him up and hug him to make the past disappear but he wasn't a cuddly child. For such a little boy, he was quite independent.

Benny had been with us about three months when Doug came home again for a few weeks. We were sitting watching television after dinner. Benny was on the floor playing with Legos. Suddenly, he shoved them away and looked up at us.

"Why can't I have someone to play with?" he asked. "It's lonely here. In India there were lots of children to play with."

"Then I think it's time for you to start school dear," I replied "You will make lots of friends there."

After I put him to bed and came downstairs, Doug was waiting.

"I've made us a cup of tea, babe." He said, indicating my favourite mug sitting on the coffee table. "Did he fall asleep okay?"

"Like always."

"I've been thinking about what he said . . . How do you feel about us finding a brother for Ben? It should be someone from his own country. Someone he can relate to."

My heart jumped with joy. I had been thinking the same thing but I wasn't sure if Doug would agree.

"Oh sweetheart, that would be wonderful. There are no neighbours with children here. When you're away, there's only him and me."

"It would have to be a boy close to his age but slightly younger. We don't want to usurp his position as our first born."

I set my tea down and crossed to Doug's chair, putting my arms around him. "My thoughts exactly."

Mantu and Benny—a few years later.

Three years later. Christopher, Mantu, Jose and Benny.

Our entire tribe. Mantu, Ben, Jose, Christopher, Anna and Chip. Whew!

EPILOGUE

I have bared my soul in my books, showing the good the bad and the ugly. We all have many facets and maybe some have more cuts (and bruises) than others.

Once we had 'cracked the nut' with Ben. The following adoptions went much faster and smoother than Ben's. Mantu, another little six year old Indian child came next. His swollen belly was the result of starvation. Like Ben, he too arrived with intestinal worms. Mantu's little legs were covered with staph sores but with a good diet, he soon recovered.

Before he arrived, we received several photos. The orphanage said they had never seen him smile except on the day he was told they had found parents for him. Ultimately, he became a lively child who never stopped smiling.

By the time Mantu arrived, I had discovered the plight of the "older" child. Most countries did not put children up for adoption after the age of thirteen. Realizing there was no time left for boys of that age, we adopted a thirteen-year-old Korean boy and, six months later, a thirteen-year-old Columbian boy.

I don't advise this for everyone, especially taking them so close together. After being abandoned and rejected for so long, these older children carry terrible scars. They no longer trust anyone and generally test the new parents to the limit, always suspicious of their motives.

Unfortunately, many such "older child" adoptions disrupt, breaking the hearts of the harried, well-meaning, would-be parents and further reinforcing the children's feelings of being unwanted.

We went through our share of turmoil and I don't know of any books published at that time that would've helped with the process. I learned through trial and error, making my share of mistakes. My one saving grace was my unbreakable commitment and, of course, the support from Doug whenever he was home.

Like all siblings, the boys fought among themselves occasionally. But they stuck together if outsiders picked on any one of them.

I abhor cigarettes but my Korean boy had smoked since age six and I could not break his habit. The more serious problems I will leave unspoken.

Once things were relatively settled with our four boys, fate again stepped in. I ended up, totally unplanned, with a three and four-year-old American brother and sister who had been wards of the state.

The three-year-old boy was classified with a mental disability; 'they' said he would never talk or be able to dress himself. Everyone wanted to take the pretty little girl but no one wanted the child with problems. I was happy to take them both and I've never regretted it. My heart warms when I look at that young boy, now a man. He definitely can dress himself and there are times I wish he wouldn't talk so much! Thank God, Social Services had enough heart not to separate them.

I knew I had reached my limit by number six. How many hours are there in a day to supervise homework, do laundry, cook and get a tribe of boys to their different sports fields for soccer practice?

I was never your typical 'PTA' mother, being a little unorthodox at times. My children did not always leap eagerly from their warm beds when I woke them at 2:00 a.m.in the morning.

"Why are you getting us up, Mum?" I remember Ben asking.

"Because we're going to Safeway to buy groceries," I replied. "The world is totally different at night. I want you to experience it."

"Do we have to?" he asked.

"Come on," I entreated. "You must have experiences. Experiences are greater than 'things'. Things get broken and lost. Experiences last a lifetime." I let my words sink in before adding, "And I'll take you to Denny's for a hot chocolate later."

When I was a new mother, I used to mentally scorn the other neighborhood mothers. As the day drew to an end and darkness began falling, they could be found out on the street, yelling for their children to come home. (The children played in a park at the end of the street.) I shuddered at the sound of their 'fishwife' voices and declared I would never lower myself to join their ranks. Being more of a lady, I bought a whistle. Of course it was made of sterling silver. Amid the screaming, fist-waving housewives, I stood alone, delicately blowing my whistle. Finding myself ignored, I blew harder and harder until my cheeks resembled a puffer fish. I'm sorry to say, before too long my voice could be heard drowning out those of my neighbors.

Occasionally, I see television documentaries about adoptive families. They all look so perfect, so happy. The children are so well-behaved and the mothers are nicely dressed with sweet smiles and modulated voices. I sigh and wish I had been perfect like that.

But then I look at my children and see how well they have turned out and I let myself off the hook. Despite that high rate of disruptions with older child adoptions, none of ours did so. We worked with WACAP on all the adoptions and I went on to do some occasional volunteer work with them later. Considering me as a success story with the older child, they asked me to interview couples who had contacted them with a view to adopting such children. My job was not to discourage them (heaven forbid) but to point out the many pitfalls and test their commitment. Nothing is sadder for all concerned than a failed adoption.

Ben was my first and therefore—my learning experience. I'm sure that was hard on him at times.

Today Ben is a chemical engineer with a loving wife and a delightful son. All our children are happy, law-abiding citizens with strong work ethics and high principles. When I think of where they would be if I hadn't taken them, I shudder. And when I think of the three biological children I lost, I tell myself, if they had lived six other children would have had no chance . . . yet violets can still make me cry.

Neither Doug nor I took children to satisfy a need in ourselves. We took them to give them love, a place to belong and a bright future. No child should have less. If, in the end, they love *us* . . . that is a blessing.

-END-

If you have enjoyed reading about my life's journey, I hope you will recommend my book and, if you are so inclined, write a review. Thank you for taking your valuable time to read my story . . . June.